SCHISM

THE MADNESS OF CROWDS, TOXICITY OF SOCIAL MEDIA, SOCIAL POLARIZATION, AND POLITICAL VIOLENCE; A CYBERNETIC APPROACH

RALPH H. ABRAHAM

SCHISM: The Madness of Crowds, Toxicity of Social Media, Social Polarization, and Political Violence; A Cybernetic Approach.

For information contact:
Epigraph Publishing Service
22 East Market Street, Suite 304
Rhinebeck, New York 12572
www.epigraphPS.com

ISBN: 978-1-960090-07-2

Bulk purchase discounts for educational or promotional purposes are available. Contact the publisher for more information.

Dedicated to my teachers:

Gregory Bateson
Rene Thom
Christopher Zeeman
Jay Forrester
Paul Lee

CONTENTS

6   Schism

PROLOGUE

From: Stephen Marche, *The Next Civil War: Dispatches from the American Future.* New York: Avid Reader Press, 2022. (Conclusion: A Note on American Hope; p. 226.)

> None of the crises described in this book are beyond the capacity of Americans to solve. It would be entirely possible for the United States to implement a modern electoral system, to restore the legitimacy of the courts, to reform its police forces, to root out domestic terrorism, to alter its tax code to address inequality, to prepare its cities and its agriculture for the effects of climate change, to regulate the mechanisms of violence. All of these futures are possible. There is one hope, however, that must be rejected outright: the hope that everything will work out by itself, that America will bumble along into better times. It won't.

This book targets the last of these seven crises: to regulate the mechanisms of violence. It's goal is to bring modern mathematics, specifically catastrophe theory, to bear on the problems of social polarization, division, and the onset of civil war in the United States of America at the time of writing, Fall 2022. We will try to connect catastrophe theory to these problems with a minimum of mathematical mystification.

Catastrophe theory

Dynamical systems theory is the branch of modern mathematics dealing with the trajectories of evolving systems. During its early days in the 1060s, it discovered chaotic behavior in these systems, so it is also known as chaos theory. Efforts to develop applications of chaos theory to the sciences in the 1970s by the mathematicians Rene Thom and Christopher Zeeman gave birth to catastrophe theory, which provides a small number of well-defined strategies for such applications.

One such application, to the outbreak of war, enjoyed a wave of popularity in the 1980s. This book is inspired by that stream of literature.

Polarization

Social and political polarization are processes of aggregation in which a population migrates into two or more subpopulations. Frequently a polarization process evolves further into tight concentrations of well separated groups, or factions or divisions. And sometimes, violent behaviors develop between two factions, leading to civil war. In American politics today, this entire sequence seems to be playing out rapidly.

The plan of this book

Our plan for this book is to locate catastrophe theory in the idea space of cybernetics, system dynamics, and the history of the mathematical modeling of social and political behavior, ending up with a three-dimensional map of the behavior of polarization, division, and the onset of civil war, and the control factors of factionalization and social media. The book has three parts.

Part A locates our work in the history of peace science, along the time-lines of early cybernetics and the system sciences, catastrophe theory, models for peace and war, the cybernetics of Norbert Wiener, the action research of David Loye, and the cultural evolution of William Irwin Thompson.

Part B begins with an optional chapter on the vocabulary of chaos theory. The main target is the notion of bifurcation, which is fundamental to this book. Then we delve into the foundational ideas of the madness of crowds, the social science of civil war, and the two control factors we have chosen for our mathematical model.

Part C concludes the book with a nontechnical description of our models for political violence and the outbreak of civil war, based on catastrophe theory.

Acknowledgments

The idea of this book derived from my obsession with the daily TV news, to which I owe a great debt, and to my many friends who consented to discuss with me the most distressing issues, most especially my wife, Ray Gwyn Smith. Larry Cuba also engaged in these difficult discussions, and graciously read the entire manuscript, suggesting many improvements. Frank Galuszka helped greatly in making connections from world problems to cybernetics.

My largest inspiration came from the pioneers of catastrophe theory, especially Chris Zeeman, who believed that mathematics could actually help in the creation of a better future for humankind and the planet.

PART A
BACKGROUND

Chapter A1
Cybernetics

Abstract

The fundamental thought style of this book is that of cybernetics. In this first chapter, we outline the history of this style from Plato to Sheldrake.

Contents

Preface

In the Fall of 1954, I left my Vermont home for the University of Michigan in Ann Arbor. Motivated by my ham radio experience, I aimed to become an electrical engineer. Norbert Wiener's 1948 book, *Cybernetics, Or Control and Communication in the Animal and the Machine* was one of the first books I read in Ann Arbor.

Our mission in this book, to understand the process of division in social systems, belongs essentially to the cognitive style of cybernetics. Thus, it is natural to begin with the history of this style, closely related to general systems theory, system dynamics, complexity theory, dynamical systems theory, nonlinear dynamics, and so on.

Of these many terms, I have chosen cybernetics as the chief representative, as it is the eldest, hence the title of this chapter. The word *cybernetics* goes back to Plato, so we may begin there and give a chronological outline of the evolution of this thought style in steps.

Plato, 380 BCE

While known primarily for his philosophy and political theory, Plato also coined the word *cybernetics* (*kybernetike*). It occurs for the first time, as far as we know, in his dialogue *Gorgias*, in which Socrates (at a dinner party) tries to define rhetoric. He says,

> I will mention for you another art which is more important than this, namely 'Kubernetike', which, just like rhetorics, saves not only people but also their bodies and goods from most extraordinary dangers.[1]

Further, in the *Republic* (375 BCE), Plato uses the term to refer to the skill of the pilot, that is, the art of navigation.[2]

Leonardo da Vinci, 1480 CE

When I arrived as a professor in the math department of UC Santa Cruz in the Fall of 1968, Fritjof Capra had just arrived as a professor in the physics department. He stayed through 1970, and later wrote:

> Those two years, 1968-1970, were the period of my life during which I experienced the most profound and most radical personal transformation.
> ... one late afternoon in 1969, my intellect and intuition came together in a profound and beautiful experience.
> ... Five years later, I summarized my findings in *The Tao of Physics*.[3]

Capra wrote on complexity and systems science in several other books, and also gave an extensive analysis of the science of Leonardo from the viewpoints of the cybernetics, systems theory, and complexity. In his book *The Science of Leonardo,* he identified Leonardo as an early precursor of these cognitive styles that have emerged on the frontiers of science in the 20th century. For example: nonlinear dynamics [6], systemic thinking [34, 169, 255], self-organization [168], complexity [169], and dynamics of complex systems [210].[4]

André-Marie Ampère, 1834

Ampère (1775-1836) was one of the founders of the science of electrodynamics. I learned of his work when I became an amateur radio operator at age 15.

The term *cybernetics* — Greek: κυβερνητική — in its scientific formulation, is due to Ampere. In 1971, Bruce Lindsay, in his article "The Larger Cybernetic", summarized the history of the term as follows:

> Later in his career (in 1834) Ampère wrote a brilliant document, "Essai sur Ie philosophie des sciences," in which he took a particularly broad view of the philosophy of science, including social and political studies as well as the better-established natural sciences, in his discussion. It was in this memoir that Ampère first introduced the term *cybernetique* to refer to the science of government. He evidently felt that this was appropriate terminology since *κυβερντεσ* is the Greek for helmsman or governor, the one who controls the direction of the ship. This may be considered the beginning of the formal recognition of the science of control, though it does not appear that Ampère's definition gained much attention in the nineteenth century, nor in our own century for that matter, until Norbert Wiener resurrected the term in his book called *Cybernetics*, published in 1948, and attempted to put the subject on a more formal basis.[5]

This word occurred in his *Essai sur la philosophie des sciences* to describe the science of civil government.

Gregory Bateson, 1936

Bateson was a few years younger than my father and died at age 76, on my 44th birthday in 1980. As an anthropologist, he did field work in the South Pacific in the 1930s. This resulted in his first book, *Naven*, of 1936, in which he introduced his idea of *schismogenesis*, a precursor of the catastrophe theory of René Thom in the 1960s. I will write more about this in a later chapter. After this he roamed over many fields in his long career, including systems theory and cybernetics.

He arrived at the University of California Santa Cruz in 1972, where I first met him in 1973. At lunch in the Catalyst cafe, we could not find much common ground, but I learned of his new book of essays, *Steps to an Ecology of Mind* (1972). The first chapter of *Part II: Form and Pattern in Anthropology* is entitled *Culture and Schismogenesis*. At this time my own research and teaching was focused on catastrophe theory, and was strongly affected by his writing.

von Bertalanffy, 1937

One of the many components or related philosophies of cybernetics is systems theory, and its modern form, called General Systems Theory (GST). This was brought to the foreground in a series of lectures by Austrian biologist Ludwig von Bertalanffy (1901-1972) beginning in 1937, and later in publications since 1946. This became a general envelope for similar theories, such as complexity, self-organization, social networks, and complex dynamical systems.

Norbert Wiener, 1943

Wiener was one year older than my father. A child prodigy of Polish Jewish parents, he earned a PhD in philosophy at age 17, a second PhD in mathematical logic at age 19, and became well-known in pure mathematics and a professor at MIT. His work on ballistics for the US military gave him a start in applied math, which he continued later during World War 2. He was among the first in the modern era to evolve cybernetic ideas. His book entitled *Cybernetics, or Control and Communication in the Animal and the Machine*, published in 1948, was the result of a decade of joint work with Dr. Arturo Rosenblueth at the Harvard Medical School and in Mexico City. An early report of this work in 1943 led to Wiener's invitation to the first Macy Conference in 1946, in which leading intellectuals of the time learned of cybernetics for the first time. His book made cybernetics a household word. A second edition in 1961 added two new chapters:

Ch. 9, On Learning and Self-Reproducing Machines, and

Ch. 10, Brain Waves and Self-Organizing Systems.

These new chapters updated cybernetics to acknowledge recent developments in computer science and artificial intelligence.

The Macy Conferences, 1946-53

The Josiah Macy. Jr. Foundation, founded by Catherine "Kate" Everit Macy in 1930 in honor of her philanthropist father, wanted to use her fortune to improve the world. She created the Macy Foundation for this purpose. Neurophysiologist Frank Fremont-Smith became its director in 1936, the year I was born. He was familiar with cybernetic concepts emerging in the theoretical biology of Conrad Waddington.

He decided to organize a series of meetings of high-level scientists from various disciplines to consider the best means of advancing science and bettering the world. An introductory meeting was organized in 1941, including Gregory Bateson, Margaret Mead, and five others. They initiated the Cybernetics Group.

A planning meeting of this group, called the Cerebral Inhibition Meeting, was convened for May 13-15, 1942. About 20 persons were invited, including Frank Fremont-Smith and Lawrence K. Frank (the organizers), Gregory Bateson, Margaret Mead, Warren McCulloch, and Arturo Rosenblueth.

The first proper meeting of the Cybernetics Group was convened at the Beekman Hotel in New York City on March 21-22, 1946. Bateson insisted that social scientists be included. The meetings continued in a regular series, known as The Macy Conferences, until 1953. Many other scientists joined the group during this period. The tenth and final meeting was on April 22-24, 1953.

In this time period the basic principles of the new field of cybernetics were laid out, as immortalized in Wiener's book of 1948.

In addition, the formal papers presented at the meetings (but not the extensive and all-important discussions) were published in five volumes, *Cybernetics. Circular Control and Feedback Mechanisms in Biological and Social Systems*, edited by Heinz von Foerster, Margaret Meade, and Hans Lukas Teuber, 1950-1955.[6]

Von Foerster was the leader of the post-Macy development of cybernetics called *second-order cybernetics*. I met him in the 1980s after he retired to the countryside not far from my home.

Margaret Mead, 1967

In a significant bifurcation in the 1960s, Margaret Mead introduced a quantum leap in cybernetics. The first-order cybernetics of the Macy conferences, at which Mead was a participant along with her then-partner Gregory Bateson, were focused on communications, control, and a strict input-output perspective of systems. In a lecture in 1967 at the founding meeting of the American Society for Cybernetics, Mead jumped up a level to consider the cybernetic practitioner/observer as a part of the system. Heinz von Foerster then popularized this idea as the cybernetics of cybernetics, or second-order cybernetics.

Further development along this line included the autopoiesis of Varela and Maturana and the conversation theory of Pask. I met Varela in 1983 at a conference in Ojai, and again in the Lindisfarne Fellowship with Bill Thompson. We had many chances to converse until his death in 2001.

René Thom, 1966

In 1960, I finished my math PhD at the University of Michigan and moved to UC Berkeley for my first job. This was very fortuitous, as Berkeley had just made a major expansion of its math department, and several important mathematicians from the international research community were in residence.

One of these was René Thom, a Fields Medalist known for his innovative work in differential topology, a new branch of mathematics. He had just begun the research which would result in catastrophe theory, the springboard for the chaos revolution a few years later. He was trying to prove a proposition of functional analysis, a classical branch of math. We worked on it together through that academic year, 1960-61, until he returned to France. Soon it was proven by Bernard Malgrange, and became known as the Malgrange Preparation Theorem, fundamental to catastrophe theory.

Parallel to the development of cybernetics as an interdisciplinary project were several other related developments, such as General Systems Theory and

Theoretical Biology (aka Systems Biology). The latter was especially a project of Conrad Waddington, who organized a series of meetings in Italy, the Serbelloni Conferences, from 1966 to 1969. René Thom attended the first of these in August 1966. As described in the following chapter, this inspired Thom to create catastrophe theory and morphogenesis, his theory of forms. The idea of morphogenesis goes back to Goethe's essay, *On morphology* of 1817.

We may regard catastrophe theory as the emergence of a strictly mathematical version of cybernetics, which was further developed by Jay Forrester.

Jay W. Forrester, 1971

Forrester was born on a farm, to which he gave credit for his expertise in systems thinking. An important computer scientist in his early career at MIT, he moved to the Sloane School of Management in 1956. There he developed *System Dynamics*, a strategy for modeling complex systems (which are networks of interacting dynamical systems) in a series of books. This became the standard method of mathematical modeling and computer simulation of such systems, still in universal use today.

William Irwin Thompson, 1973

In the summer of 1984, an extraordinary conference was organized at the Ojai Foundation in Ojai, California. Called the *Way of the Warrior*, it was the occasion of my meeting a number of systems thinkers who later became important to me, including: Andra Akers, Gigi Coyle, Adele Getty, Joan Halifax, Francis Huxley, R.D. Laing, Deena Metzger, and Francisco Varela.

Andra Akers, an actress from Hollywood, was inspired by the conference to create a salon, lecture series, and institute, the International Synergy Institute (ISI). There I met more individuals who became important to me, including David Dunn, Hazel Henderson, Stan Tenen, and Bill Thompson.

Thompson, a cultural historian and poet, had abandoned his professorship at MIT in 1973 to direct the Lindisfarne Association as a residential commune and discussion group of systems thinkers devoted to the evolution of planetary culture active until 2012.

Bill became interested in chaos theory, and in 1986 I was inducted into the association. Then I met more individuals who became important to me, including: Gregory Bateson, Mary Catherine Bateson, Wesley Jackson, Stuart Kaufmann, James Lovelock, Rusty Schweickart, Brother David Steindl-Rast, John Todd, and Sim van der Ryn.

A veritable volcano of intellectual support stemmed from a single conference in 1984. And one significant derivative of this support was my first book on the application of chaos theory to world cultural history, *Chaos, Gaia, Eros*. As I was writing this in 1988, I sought feedback from Bill Thompson about my proposed division of world cultural history and prehistory into three epochs. He told me that he had published a similar framework in his book, *Pacific Shift*, of 1985.

The Lindisfarne Association stimulated a plethora of mutual entangled conferences, books, papers, lectures, and videos, all devoted to the creation of a viable future for global civilization.

Rupert Sheldrake, 1981

We usually think of cybernetics as cyber-netics, that is, a

theory of networks: nodes connected by node-to-node links. However, networks may also be linked by an ambient field that radiates information from one node to many others.

Stimulated by Goethe's writings on the morphology of plants in the 1790s, the concept of a radiating field evolved in the history of biological science. A morphogenetic field is thought to carry information on form from plant to plant, or from cell to cell.

The phrase *morphogenetic field* first appeared in a paper of Alexander A. Gurwitsch (1874-1954) in 1922. Gurwitsch, a Jewish scientist much interested in music, was a colleague of Vladimir Vernadsky, the pioneer of Biospherics, and a good friend of Hans Driesch, a pioneer of vitalism.

The field idea also occurred in the writings of Paul Alfred Weiss (1898-1989), also a Jewish scientist influenced by music, in 1926. Weiss pioneered the systems view in biology, along with Ludwig von Bertalanffy.

The early thinking on this field idea in biology was greatly extended by Rupert Sheldrake in his first book, *A New Science of Life,* of 1981. In the Introduction, he has written,

> The concept of morphogenetic fields can be of practical scientific value only if it leads to testable predictions which differ from those of the conventional mechanistic theory. And such predictions cannot be made unless morphogenetic fields are considered to have measurable effects.
>
> The hypothesis put forward in this book is based on the idea that morphogenetic fields do indeed have measurable physical effects. It proposes that specific morphogenetic fields are responsible for the characteristic form and organization of systems at all levels of complexity, not only in the realm of

biology, but also in the realms of chemistry and physics. ...

This hypothesis, called the hypothesis of formative causation, leads to an interpretation of many physical and biological phenomena which is radically different from that of existing theories ...

In this book, Sheldrake acknowledges Gurwitsch, Weiss, and Waddington for their contributions to morphogenesis and the systems view of biology.

In the intervening 40 years, Sheldrake has produced a plethora of books and articles reporting scores of experiments in support of the hypothesis of formative causation.

Conclusion

There are many developments in the systems thinking style: general systems, general evolution, system dynamics, dynamical systems, complex dynamical systems, chaos, cybernetics, autopoiesis, synergetics, adaptive systems, catastrophes, the sciences of complexity, and so on.

I have adopted the name cybernetics for this entire evolutionary trajectory, which deserves an extensive genealogical treatment. But here I have given just a bare beginning, based upon my own involvement from 1960 on.

The following chapters will unpack some of these theories.

Notes

1   *Gorgias*, Stephens, p. 211.
2   *Republic*, Book I, Stephens, p. 431.
3   Abraham, Ralph H. (2019), pp. 138-139.
4   The numbers in brackets indicate page numbers in (Capra, 2007).
5   Quoted in http://www.eoht.info/page/Cybernetics.
6   Republished in (Pias, 2016). Of the 10 conferences, only the final 5 are included.

Chapter A2
Schismogenesis

Abstract

Catastrophe is a word in the jargon of mathematics. And *schismogenesis* comes from anthropology. Here is a history of these concepts, with particular attention to the years 1933 to 1978. This expands the story of cybernetics in the preceding chapter.

Contents

Foreword

Catastrophe is the underlying mathematical idea of many of my writings. This concept is also known by other names, such as saltatory leap, major transformation, morphogenesis, or schismogenesis. Here I will lay out its origins, beginning with René Thom, 1972. A later chapter provides a concise (and optional) introduction to the mathematical theory underlying catastrophe theory.

Catastrophe Theory

Dynamical system theory is a new branch of mathematics dealing with the motion, or dynamic, determined by an evolutionary rule in a *state space*, a space of virtual states of a system. Our context is a system to be modeled. Each point in the state space is regarded as the identifier of state of the target system.

Catastrophe theory is a style for the application of dynamical systems theory to the sciences, set by René Thom in his classic text, *Structural Stability and Morphogenesis: An Outline of a General Theory of Models*, originally published in French in 1972. The English translation by David Fowler, updated by Thom, appeared in 1973.

The basic ideas were set down in the introduction of Thom's book. I may paraphrase them here.

The state space, the space of all possible states of the target system, is a geometric object, M, which locally looks like Euclidean rectilinear space, but globally may be curved and twisted. For our purpose, an exposition of some exemplary models due to Zeeman, we may take this to be a Euclidean space: a line, a plane, or a three-dimensional space, as in high-school geometry.

The *dynamic* is a *vectorfield*, that is an assignment of a velocity vector to each and every point of *M*. As such, it has a dynamical behavior which is understood by dynamical systems theory in terms of its portrait, a map of its attractors, basins, and separatrices.

Next, there is another manifold, let's say a line, a plane, or three-dimensional space, *C*, called the *control space*. We must imagine a dynamic on the state space, *X(c)*, defined for every point *c* in the control space.

Finally, there is a set, *K*, within *C*, called the *catastrophe set*. When the control point, *c*, moves across the catastrophe set, *K*, the portrait of the dynamic, *X(c)*, undergoes substantial change: a morphogenesis, or bifurcation, or catastrophe, occurs.

In the application of the theory to world cultural history, the control space is the timeline of history. All this will become clearer in the context of examples to come.

Catastrophe theory was greatly popularized by Christopher Zeeman in the 1970s in a collection of carefully elaborated examples.

The Bifurcation Perspective

A bifurcation along the timeline of history is sometimes called a *schism*, or major cultural transformation. *Schismogenesis*, the development of a schism, is a bifurcation event in history.

In this context historical time is the scale on which bifurcation events are located. The largest bifurcations are sparsely placed on the timeline. For example, the acquisition of language, or the agricultural revolution. Between any two of these large events there may be interpolated some number of medium-sized events. And between any two of these, some smaller ones, and so on.

The collection of all these significant times in history is called the bifurcation set. This set of times may be very large, so we may be unable to catalog them all.

The Genesis of the Catastrophe Concept

Here is a concise version of catastrophic historiography, the view of world cultural history seen as a series of major transformations.[1]

There is an ancient background, including the four yugas of Ancient India, and the four ages of Ancient Egypt and Classical Greece. Here are some of the leading authors of catastrophic historiography from 1000 to 1930:

1000, Al-Biruni (Iranian polymath)
1197, Joachim de Fiora (Italian theologian)
1377, Ibn Khaldun (Arab philosopher)
1697, Gottfried Leibniz (German polymath)
1725, Giambattista Vico (Italian philosopher)
1855, Herbert Spenser (English philosopher)
1860, Jacob Burckhardt (Swiss cultural historian)
1911, William Flinders Petrie (English Egyptologist)
1917, Oswald Spengler (German world historian)

Al-Biruni wrote of historical eras — the division of history into segments divided by bifurcations.— In his work *The Chronology of Ancient Nations*.

Joachim de Fiora divided history into three epochs, of the Father, the Son, and the Holy Spirit.

Ibn Khaldun founded historiography with his work, *Muqaddimah*. Here he introduced the fundamental ideas of the beginning, development, and the fall of all societies.

Gottfried Leibniz indulged in a project of universal history, seeking the origins and migrations of peoples.

Giambattista Vico proposed a theory of cultural evolution and cycles of history.

Herbert Spenser founded social Darwinism, in which societies evolve according to rules similar to those of biological evolution.

Jacob Burckhardt was among the founders of cultural history. With art history as a model, he identified cultural epochs such as the Renaissance, and Modernity.

William Flinders Petrie developed the archeological method of dating layers based on pottery styles.

Oswald Spengler showed how cultures grow and decline in analogy with human beings.

The Development of the Catastrophe View

The expansion of the catastrophe view from history to larger spheres and the whole of epistemology were begun by Ludwik Fleck. I will begin my detailed chronology with him and tell five crucial stories:

1933, Ludwik Fleck (1896-1961)
1934, Arnold Toynbee (1989-1975)
1935, Gregory Bateson (1904-1980)
1962, Thomas Kuhn (1922–1996)
1966, René Thom (1923-2002)

1933, Ludwik Fleck (1896-1961)

Life. Fleck, a Polish Jew, was born in Lvov, Poland. He received his MD there in 1922, and began a lifetime of medical research. Initially he studied typhus and virology in

Lvov, then microbacteriology in Lvov and Vienna. He became an erudite humanist, and wrote his first philosophical paper in 1927, *Some Specific Features of the Medical Way of Thinking*. He developed his original theory of thought styles and thought collectives in 1933, which was published in German in 1935. In that year he was dismissed from his position as head of a bacteriological laboratory in Lvov under the anti-Jewish measures of the time, and continued in Lvov in private practice. He discovered important serological methods, especially regarding the Wasserman antibody test for syphilis. Lvov was captured by the Germans in 1941, and Fleck was resettled to the Lvov ghetto, then deported to Auschwitz, and then to Buchenwald, which was liberated in 1945. Fleck then resettled in Lublin, Poland. In 1957, he emigrated to Israel, where he died in 1961.[2]

Ideas. Fleck's book on his original theory was written in 1933. The English translation of 1979 by Fred Bailey and Thaddeus J. Trent, was entitled, *Genesis and Development of a Scientific Fact*. This was a founding contribution to the sociology of science. The Prologue, written in 1934, begins with the question, *What is a fact?*

His answer was: A fact is a consensus, the result of a social process among a thought collective, that is, a community of minds with a common thought style. The collective is more-or-less defined by the shared thought style. He is interested in the interaction of distinct thought styles, and the development of a thought style. A historical line of development may have discontinuities, which are sometimes accompanied by the genesis of a new fact.

His main example was the Wasserman test for syphilis:

Once a structurally complete and closed system

of opinions consisting of many details and relations has been formed, it offers enduring resistance to anything that contradicts it.

A striking example of this tendency is given by our history of the concept of "carnal scourge" [syphilis] in its prolonged endurance against every new notion. What we are faced with here is not so much simple passivity or mistrust of new ideas as an active approach which can be divided into several stages.

(1) A contradiction to the system appears unthinkable.

(2) What does not fit into the system remains unseen;

(3) alternatively, if it is noticed, either it is kept secret, or

(4) laborious efforts are made to explain an exception in terms that do not contradict the system.

(5) Despite the legitimate claims of contradictory views, one tends to see, describe, or even illustrate those circumstances which corroborate current views and thereby give them substance.[3]

And later he wrote:

All empirical discovery can therefore be construed as supplement, development, or transformation of the thought style.[4]

Here, Fleck distinguished between gradual and sudden transformations, anticipating the mathematical theory of bifurcation of the 1960s. This mathematical theory distinguished three sorts of transformation: gradual, explosive, and catastrophic.

Although described his ideas in the context of microbiology and medical science, Fleck foresaw their application throughout epistemology:

> We see professional and semiprofessional thought communities in commerce, the military, sports, art, politics, fashion, science, and religion.[5]

This was certainly the case in my experience of the birth of chaos theory in the math community in the 1960s. A schism developed between the experimental and the purely theoretical approaches to the chaos idea. The worldwide math research community divided into two disparate groups — the experimentalists and the purists — and communication between the groups broke down.

1934, Arnold Toynbee (1989-1975)

Life. Toynbee was born in London and educated at Oxford, where he taught ancient history from 1912 to 1915. After a stint in the British Foreign Office, he taught modern Greek and Byzantine studies at University London until 1921. He resumed academic work at the London School of Economics in 1925.

Toynbee was among the most read scholars of his time. *A Study of History,* published 1934-1961 in 12 volumes by Oxford University Press, is his best-known work.

Ideas. A quick look into his thought is provided by the chapter titles of his main work:

> Vol I: Introduction; The Geneses of Civilizations

Vol II: The Geneses of Civilizations
Vol III: The Growths of Civilizations
Vol IV: The Breakdowns of Civilizations
Vol V: The Disintegrations of Civilizations, I
Vol VI: The Disintegrations of Civilizations, II
Vol VII: Universal States; Universal Churches
Vol VIII: Heroic Ages; Contacts between Civilizations in Space
Vol IX: Contacts between Civilizations in Time; Law and Freedom in History; The Prospects of the Western Civilization
Vol X: The Inspirations of Historians; A Note on Chronology
Vol XI: Historical Atlas and Gazetteer (with Edward D. Myers)
Vol XII: Reconsiderations

In summary, Toynbee ...

... examined the rise and fall of 26 civilizations in the course of human history, and he concluded that they rose by responding successfully to challenges under the leadership of creative minorities composed of elite leaders.[6]

Toynbee's suggestion for the trigger of historical transformations — minority leaders — became controversial, and his influence on later historians declined. In the case of the MeToo and Black Lives Matters movements of today, his suggestion has been validated: each movement was triggered by a few charismatic leaders.

1935, Gregory Bateson (1904-1980)

Life. Bateson, born in Cambridgeshire, was the son of the geneticist, William Bateson. He earned a PhD in anthropology from Cambridge University in 1929, and did field work in New Guinea and Bali before World War 2. He was a founding member of the Macy Conferences, 1941-53, from which the field of cybernetics evolved. He came to the United States in the 1950s, and taught at UC Santa Cruz from 1972 until retirement. I met him there in 1974, as he was moving into the house I had been renting. In 1976 he was appointed a regent of the UC system.

Ideas. Following his field work with the Iatmul tribe in New Guinea, he wrote a field report of sorts as his first book, *Naven,* in 1936. Naven is an Iatmul word referring to a tribal ritual which is the main topic of the report. In this ritual, men and women exchange clothing and behaviors.

An entire chapter of 26 pages, Chapter 13, is devoted to the introduction of his novel concept of schismogenesis, which derived from his analysis of the Naven ceremony. In a prior article, *Culture Contact and Schismogenesis,* originally published in the journal *Man* in 1935 (and reprinted in his book *Steps to an Ecology of Mind* of 1972) he introduced *schismogenesis* as a synonym for *progressive differentiation.*[7] In the language of chaos theory, in the mathematics of the 1960s, this would be considered a *subtle bifurcation.*

In 1936, Bateson wrote:

> I would define schismogenesis *as a process of differentiation in the norms of individual behavior resulting from cumulative interaction between individuals.*[8]

This is specific to his field of anthropology. Bateson, a social anthropologist, characterized cultures in terms of behavioral norms. Cumulative interactions between individuals diverge in a circular process of adjustment of norms.

But following Bateson's participation in the Macy conferences and the origins of cybernetics, he broadened his scope. In 1958, in a new Epilogue to the second edition of *Naven*, he wrote:

> It seems to me, today, that there is a partial answer to these problems [of epistemology] in the processes of schismogenesis which are analyzed in this book [*Naven*], but this partial answer could hardly be extracted from that analysis when the book was written. These further steps had to wait upon other advances, such as the expansion of learning theory, the development of cybernetics, the application of Russell's Theory of Logical Types to communication theory, and Ashby's formal analysis of those orders of events which must lead to parametric change in previously steady-state systems.
>
> A discussion of the relationship between schismogenesis and these more modern developments of theory is therefore a first step toward a new synthesis.[9]

We see that by 1958 Bateson had advanced from Toynbee's limited proposal of 1934 for the development of a schism in response to a challenge, to a more detailed transactional process involving cybernetics.

1962, Thomas Kuhn (1922–1996)

Life. Born in Cincinnati, Ohio, Kuhn obtained his PhD in physics from Harvard in 1949. After being denied tenure at Harvard, he became a very influential philosopher of science. He joined the faculty of UC Berkeley in 1956, as I did in 1960, but we did not meet there. Then he moved to the faculty of Princeton University in 1964, as I did also, from Columbia University. We occasionally had lunch together in the student cafeteria.

Ideas. In 1957 he published his first book, *The Copernican Revolution.* Here he dissected in detail the major transformation in astronomical world-view occasioned by Copernicus, and evolved his notion of *paradigm shift.* This was followed in 1962 by his best known work, *The Structure of Scientific Revolutions.*

He developed a theory of paradigm shift, in which epochs of constant paradigm were punctuated by shifts caused by the accumulation of anomalies, in which observations conflict with the current paradigm. These anomalous results accumulate into a crisis, and if a rival paradigm comes into view, the shift is triggered.

Kuhn's idea of paradigm shift is similar to Ludwik Fleck's prior concept of the development of a thought-style. In fact, Kuhn read Fleck's book in 1949 or 1950, while still at Harvard. And in his Foreword to the second edition of Fleck's book, Kuhn wrote:

> I have more than once been asked what I took from Fleck and can only respond that I am almost totally uncertain. Surely I was reassured by the existence of his book, a nontrivial contribution be-cause in 1950 and for some years thereafter I knew of no one else who saw in the history of science

what I myself was finding there.[10]

So Kuhn was inspired by his reading of Fleck, but he goes further in analyzing the shift process as resulting from an accumulation of evidential forces.

1966, René Thom (1923-2002)

Life. Thom was born in Montbéliard, in the Northeast of France, near the Swiss Border. He received the PhD in 1951 from the University of Paris. We met at UC Berkeley in 1960, where we worked together on outstanding problems of differential topology, he was a professor at the University of Strasbourg. In 1964 he joined the Institut des hautes études scientifiques (IHES) outside Paris as a founding professor, where we met again in 1967.

Ideas. Following the development of cobordism theory (a new branch of differential topology) begun in his PhD thesis, for which he received the Fields Medal in 1958, Thom went on in 1960 to develop the theory of stratified sets, another new branch of differential topology. In 1966, in Princeton, I began to receive letters from Thom on his emerging ideas of catastrophe theory, with proposed applications to linguistics and to quantum theory. This project eventually became a book, *Stabilité structurelle et morphogénèse*, published by my publisher, William Benjamin, in 1972.[11]

An excellent English translation by David Fowler was brought out in 1975, also by Benjamin.[12] This was more than a translation. It greatly clarified the difficult ideas of Thom and launched the subject into a trajectory which lasted for several years, and affected the history of several sciences and philosophies. This trajectory was further boosted by the splendid writings of E. C. Zeeman, developing applications of the theory to various fields, first in an article in the *Scientific American* of 1976, and then in a thick and readable book in 1977.[13] Among these applications were aggressive behavior, stock market crashes, anorexia nervosa, phase transitions, and oscillations.

Zeeman's book includes, as Chapter 3, a model for the heart beat and nerve impulse, showing how to adapt catastrophe theory to a periodic behavior, like the heart beat. Zeeman's crucial idea here was a mapping of the geometric substrate of the phenomena.

For example, the shape of the heart is mapped into the mathematical model for the catastrophic behavior of a single cell of heart muscle. The model for the single heart cell is a folded surface in three-dimensional space. Each cell of the heart muscle is interpreted as a point on this folded surface. An external force, the heart pacemaker, slides this heart image along the folded surface. When the heart image slides over the fold, a contraction moves down the heart muscle, pumping blood.

In the Spring and Summer of 1969, the Maths Research Centre of the University of Warwick in Coventry, created by Zeeman, had just opened. An international conference on Dynamical Systems Theory was taking place, at which I was an invited participant.

The heart action model of Zeeman was a great stimulus for my own attempts to model consciousness, which depends on vibrations. I noted this connection in my journal on July 31, 1969, while I was attending the conference.

The Birth of Catastrophe Theory

I learned of catastrophe theory from Thom in 1966. He had

then a great interest in algebraic geometry, and had made a
theory of stratified sets which generalize algebraic varieties, an
important topic of algebraic geometry. He had an acute visual
ability, and it occurred to him that these figures might be the
basis for a universal theory of forms, like Plato's. He began
looking for applications for some of these sets which appear in
three-dimensional space.

Some of the areas in which he was searching, included
in his letters to me of 1966, were from quantum mechanics,
astrophysics, biological morphogenesis, animal behavior, and
linguistics.

Meanwhile, Conrad Waddington (1905-1975), a
developmental biologist at the University of Edinburgh,
became interested in organicism, an idea for overcoming the
dichotomy between materialism and vitalism in theoretical
biology.[14] A great organizer, he obtained funding from the
Rockefeller Foundation for a series of four conferences at the
Foundation's property, the Villa Serbelloni, on Lake Como.

At the first of these conferences, in August 1966, Thom
was present. He and Waddington had inspirational talks. In a
report of the first two meetings, Waddington wrote:

> The facts that in normal development only a
> limited number of different cell types put in an ap-
> pearance, and that each of them shows some power
> of "regulation" or resistance to disturbing effects of
> the environment, indicate that we are dealing with a
> number of domains of phase space, each containing
> a vector field dominated by a particular attractor.
> In the context of development we have to think of
> these attractors as extended in the time dimension.
> The fact that the vector fields converge onto the
> attractors gives rise to a process of "homeorhesis",

which can be contrasted with the more convention-
al idea of homeostasis in which the vector fields
converge on to a static point which is not time-extended.[15] I have proposed the name "chreod" for
such a multidimensional domain which contains
a vector field converging on to a time-extended
attractor.

This notion was developed in a way which was
both more generalized and more precisely formu-
lated by the French topologist, René Thom. He
pointed out that the concept can be used over a
much wider field than that of embryonic development; for example, the field of the shades of meaning of a word can be regarded as a chreod dominated by the attractor which is its "concise dictionary"
meaning. Again, at the second meeting Richard
Gregory discussed a theory of perception under the
provocative title "How so little information controls
so much ". His answer was, roughly, that a small
amount of information arriving through the sense
organs activates "pre-existing" models in the brain
— which can be otherwise expressed by saying that
the incoming information falls within the domain
of a certain chreod and thus converges on to its
attractor.

The main feature of the discussions in this area,
however, was an analysis by Thom of the "catastrophes" at which the organization controlling one
domain breaks down and the system becomes
switched into one or more alternatives. Physical
examples are a shock wave, a liquid jet breaking
up into drops, a wave breaking. He claims to have
shown that in real four-dimensional space there are

only seven possible types of elementary catastrophe.[16]

Here we find the origin of Thom's applications of catastrophe
theory to biology, and also, Waddington's identification of his
chreod with the forms of Thom's catastrophe theory.

The Demise of Catastrophe Theory

The theory of Thom included simple catastrophes, which
were much studied and applied, especially by Zeeman, due to
their relative simplicity. But these had a serious limitation, in
that they applied only to static attractors. Thus, systems with
periodic or chaotic attractors (discovered in 1961) could not
be accommodated. As chaos theory rose, catastrophe theory
declined. This decline was largely due to the opposition of
some very influential mathematicians, such as Steve Smale,
who wrote a devastating review of Zeeman's 1977 book in
1978.

Notes

1   For a longer account see (Abraham, 1988.)
2   For excellent biography see (Fleck, 1935/1979).
3   See (Fleck, 1935; p. 27).
4   See (Fleck, 1979; p. 92). The original is italicized.
5   See (Fleck, 1979; p. 107).
6   From the *Encyclopedia Britannica*.
7   See (Bateson, 1972; p. 68).
8   See (Bateson, 1936; p. 175).
9   See (Bateson, 1958; p. 284) or equally (Bateson, 1991; p. 52).
10   See (Fleck 1979; p. xiii).
11   Morphogenesis, as used by Thom, is a mathematical version of schismogenesis.
12   (Zeeman/Fowler, 1975)
13   (Zeeman, 1977)
14   See (Peterson, 2016; Introduction).
15   Homeostasis, a static equilibrium, was long considered the normal state of a living system. Waddington, recognizing the dynamical patterns in Nature, coined the terms "homeorhesis" and "chreod" to facilitate the discussion of dynamics in biology.
16   See (Waddington, 1968; p. 526).

CHAPTER A3
ERODYNAMICS AND THE DISCHAOTIC PERSONALITY

Dedicated to: Kurt Lewin, 1890-1947
and Gregory Bateson, 1904-1980

Abstract

The binary dichotomy of chaos/dischaos is used in place of that of disorder/order in modeling the psyche in the style of Kurt Lewin. Application is made to several ideas of Gregory Bateson.

Publication

Ms #76, written March 22, 1993. Not previously published.

Contents

Historical Introduction

The new field of erodynamics consists of applications of the mathematical theories of dynamics, chaos, and bifurcations to models in the social sciences, including economics. Here we give a capsule history of the field. Complex dynamical systems theory provides a new modeling strategy for social systems, which are usually too complex to model without a theory that allows chaos and bifurcation. These new models contribute to the hermeneutical circle for evolving social structures, in which mathematical help in understanding may be very welcome. Even the simplest social systems, such as two persons or two nations, tax our intuitive cognitive strategies. Dynamical models may be used as navigational aids for cooperation or conflict resolution in many situations in which good will prevails, yet does not suffice.

An early dynamical model for social systems, the first we know of, is the (1837) Verhulst model for population growth. Later, in the context of the Great War, came Lanchester's (1914) model for war, and Richardson's (1919) model for the arms race. Next came dynamical models for economic systems, with Keynes, Schumpeter, and von Neumann in the 1930s. Rashevsky, the founder or mathematical biology and editor or Richardson's papers, invented mathematical sociology during World War II. This sequence accelerated after World War II with the syntheses of general systems theory and cybernetics. In the mathematical branch of these movements, systems dynamics, we have the extensive development or models for factories, cities, nations, the world monetary system, and many other complex systems. The work of Jay Forrester was central to this growth. The independent development of dynamical systems theory after Poincaré remained aloof from social applications until recently, and now a reunion of these two branches of mathematics is underway. In the Poincaré lineage came the development of applied singularity theory by René Thom, its extensive application to social systems (as catastrophe theory) by Christopher Zeeman, and new dynamical models for economic systems by Radnor, Smale, and Chichilnisky in the 1970s. Since then, chaos theory has discovered systems with complex structure; and systems dynamics has discovered chaos.

The Pioneers

Here are some milestones in the evolution of erodynamics.

Lanchester, 1914

Frederick William Lanchester (1868-1946) was an English engineer. A creative genius interested in economics, physics, military strategy, automobiles, and airplanes, he was of one of the first to grasp the military advantage of aircraft. In this context, he conceived a dynamical model for armed conflict, in which numerical strength, firepower, strategy, and attitude were counted (Lanchester, 1914).

Richardson, 1919

Lewis Frye Richardson (1881-1953) was an English physicist, meteorologist, and Quaker. A conscientious objector in World War I, he served as an ambulance driver on the front lines in France, and saw a great deal of death and suffering. He decided to devote his life to the elimination of war. He developed a linear model for the arms race between two nations, in which a spiral of increasing armaments of

each nation resulted from mathematical laws. He felt that
the individual nations caught in this kind of dynamic were
innocent victims of an out-of-control global system. He
submitted a paper on this model to a journal, fully confident
that another war could be averted. However, the paper was
rejected, and the second World War began. After this rejection
Richardson continued his work, trying to justify the model
on the basis of actual armament statistics. In this effort, he
founded the field of politicometrics. Richardson's life work
was published posthumously in 1960.

Von Neumann, 1932

The word *economics* is derived from the Greek *oikos nomos*,
meaning the management of a household. This is also, by
the way, the source of oikonomia, the Christian doctrine
of the economy of salvation. In the last century, economics
became an important social science. Because economics
is naturally equipped with numerical data, it was one of
the first of the social sciences to receive a mathematical
treatment. In 1932 John von Neumann (1903-1957) created
one of the first dynamical models for an economic system,
giving rise to a whole industry of mathematical analyses,
computer simulations, and data collection (econometrics) (see
Goodwin, 1991, Chap. 3).

Bateson, 1935

Gregory Bateson (1904-1980) adapted the Richardson
arms race model to the process of the division of a culture
into subcultures, analogous to differentiation in biological
systems. He called this universal dynamical process for
the development of a schism a Richardsonian process of

schismogenesis (Bateson, 1972, p. 68). In fact, schismogenesis, a social form of bifurcation, was one of Bateson's main themes (Bateson, 1972, pp. 61, 107). Later he would apply it to schizophrenia (see "The Double Bind" below).

Lewin, 1936

Kurt Lewin (1890-1947) was influenced by the hermeneutics of Dilthey, with whom he had contact in Berlin,and Wertheimer, who had developed a *field* concept in Gestalt psychology early in 1923. This was extensively developed by Lewin. His *life space* is a sort of psychological field, extending over a group of animals (Lewin, 1951/1975). He modeled social psychological objects by shapes within the life space, or field. He also introduced concepts of dynamics and bifurcations in these shapes, under the name *topological psychology* (Lewin, 1936). The rigorous development of Lewin's ideas had to await complex dynamical systems theory, or chaos theory, in the 1960s and 1970s.

Rashevsky, 1939

Nicholas Rashevsky (1895-1964) escaped from the Russian revolution to become the indefatigable pioneer of mathematical biology at the University of Chicago (Karreman, 1990). He published an early erodynamics paper (1939) and a book (1947) applying the methods of mathematical biology to sociology. He edited the writings of Lewis Frye Richardson, the founder of erodynamics, for posthumous publication in 1960. In *Looking at History through Mathematics* (Rashevsky, 1968), he offers steps toward a mathematical model for Arnold Toynbee's theory of history. A tentative prevision of catastrophe theory is included to explain revolutions:

Whenever we have threshold phenomena,
whether in physical, biological, or social systems,
the configuration of the system at the moment
when the threshold is reached becomes unstable
and the slightest, even infinitesimal, displacement
of the configuration in a proper direction leads
eventually to a finite change in the configuration of
the system. Therefore, a change in the behavior of a
single individual, no matter how small, may precip-
itate in an unstable social configuration, a process
that leads to a finite, sometimes radical, change.
(Rashevsky, 1968, p. 119)

Also, an explicit recognition of the hermeneutic circle is
presented in the Preface of this book, as part of an extensive
defense of mathematical modeling.

Jung,1952

Carl G. Jung (1875-1961) came late in his life to an
awakening, expressed in his book *Answer to Job* (1952). This
presents an astonishingly bold psychoanalysis; of the god
Yahweh, in which good and evil are combined in a fractal
binary. Further, his concept of *enantiodromia* (oscillation)
admits a Lewinian model (Abraham, Abraham, & Shaw, 1990,
pp. III-11 ff.).

Thom, 1972

In the 1960s René Thom developed catastrophe theory; he
published the theory in 1972, along with a number of ideas
for its application in the sciences, linguistics, philosophy, etc.

The final chapter of this work sets out the modern formulation of erodynamics in the context of proposed applications to sociology and psychology.

Zeeman, 1976

In the 1970s Carlos lsnard and Christopher Zeeman replaced the linear model of Lewis Richardson and Gregory Bateson with a nonlinear model, the cusp catastrophe of Thom's theory. They applied their model to the original arms race context of Richardson's work, showing how the model fit a situation of schismogenesis, in which the voting population of a democratic nation split into hawks and doves. Zeeman also adapted the cusp to model anorexia nervosa, an emotional disease in which phases of gluttony and fasting alternate (Postle, 1980; Zeeman, 1977).

Kushelman/Kadyrov, 1985

Mark Kushelman (under the pseudonym Kadyrov), a mathematician and systems' scientist then in Moscow, put together two of these cusp models into a double-cusp model for two nations engaged in an arms race, completing the nonlinear version of Richardson's original model. It provides a map, in the two-dimensional space of sensitivities of each nation to armaments of the other, showing regions of different behaviors, such as hawks and hawks, hawks and doves, doves and hawks, and doves and doves. Surprisingly, in the north-west and south-east sectors of this map, Kushelman found oscillating behavior. This might be significant in situations of codependence or addictive behavior (Abraham, Mayer-Kress, Keith, & Koebbe, 1991). A slightly different double cusp map was used by Callahan and Sashin (1987) in the treatment of anorexia nervosa and affect-response. Some other nonlinear adaptations of Richardson's model for the arms race have been studied by Saperstein and Mayer-Kress (1988), who found chaotic behavior in their model.

Haraway, 1985

In *Manifesto for Cyborgs*, Donna Haraway (1985) analyzes the cyborg, an integral being who is part human, part machine. Without explicit reference to fractal geometry, Haraway's vision is essentially fractal. She describes three critical cases of the fractal deconstruction of a binary: human/animal, animal-human/machine, and physical/nonphysical. She extends these examples to a long list of fractured identities: self/other, mind/body, culture/nature, male/female, and so on, of political significance. This path-finding analysis leads the way to a fractal method for the deconstruction of all binaries as well as to the reconstruction of self-images (and scientific categories) as fractal identities. 'Thus, she introduced fractal geometry into anthropology, beginning a transformation which is ongoing today. Since 1985, there has been an erodynamic explosion (See also Eglash, 1992).

Dischaos: Dynamical Models

The fractal concept introduced into anthropology by Haraway and subsequent works by Wagnar, McWhinney, and Strathern is epitomized by the idea of the sandy beach. We begin the description of our model by recalling this static concept, then extending it to the dynamical model of Lewin, Thom, and Zeeman as the fractal separatrix or basin boundary (Fig. 11.1). Finally we will use the model to introduce the concept of the dischaotic personality.

The Sandy Beach

In Benoit Mandelbrot's classic text, the second chapter is titled, "How long is the coast of Britain?" We will describe the sandy beach in the two-dimensional context of a map. Thus, the ocean and the land are mostly two-dimensional Before fractal geometry, the map showed the boundary between the ocean and the land as a smooth curve, a one-dimensional coast. But now, thanks to Mandelbrot (he gives credit to Richardson), we may zoom in on the coast and see that it has vary small islands, even pebbles, in a densely packed structure. Zooming in again, we see grains of sand on the beach, and in the ocean close to the beach. All this is the coast: It has a fractal dimension. Land penetrates into the ocean in a frothy structure of sand; ocean penetrates into the land in a frothy structure of water in the wet sand. Not only is the coast a fractal with a dimension more than one but less than two, but it is a fractal region: the coastal zone. The ocean and land are not divided by the roast in a binary fashion; they interpenetrate in a fractal geometry. The fractals of chaos theory — attractors, separatrices, and bifurcations — are all of the sandy beach variety.

Fractal Separatrices

We now make a jump to the dynamical model of Lewin (1936), who imagined the life space or psychological field of a person as the state space of a (continuous) dynamical system. The observable behaviors of this model are the attractors, and the significant regions of life space, then, are the basins of attraction of these attractors. Further, the separatrices (the boundaries of these basins) are crucial to the Lewinian view

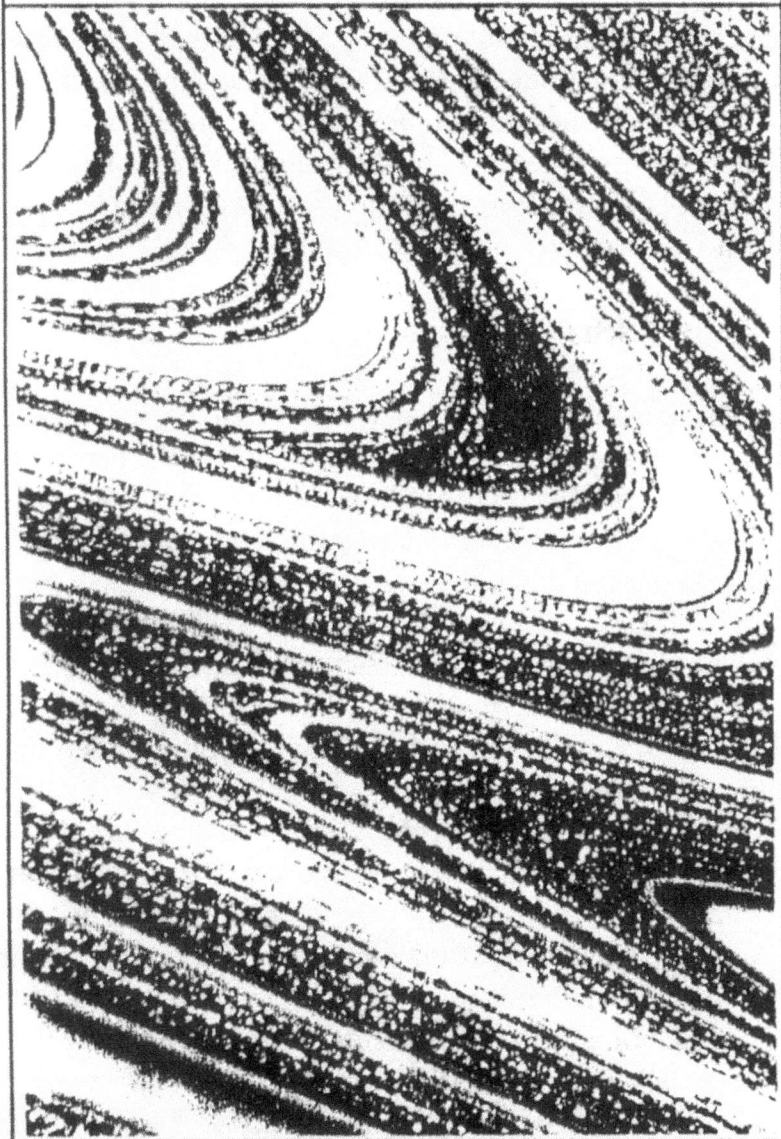

Figure 11.1: Fractal Separatrix
Formed by coupled oscillators, and seen in Poincaré section.
(Grebogi, Ott, Varosi, & Yorke, "Fractal Basin Boundary 2," displayed at an exhibit at the Fine Arts Museum of Long Island, April 1-June 24, 1990.)

of psychology (Abraham, Abraham, & Shaw, 1990). In many important examples, these separatrices are fractal (Kennedy & Yorke, 1991; Ueda, 1992). This means that the sandy beach concept applies to the boundary between two different behavioral regions. This will be our basic model in this chapter. We should point out, however, that the improvement of the Lewinian model due to Thom and Zeeman is more complex: the attractor-basin portrait in the state space (life space of Lewin) is replaced by the response diagram, in the product of the state space and the control space of a dynamical scheme (morphogenetic field of Thom).

The Dischaotic Personality

We now assume a Lewinian dynamical model for the self or life space of an individual. Different aspects of the personality, depending critically on the individual, are represented in this model by group; of basins of attraction. These may be slowly changing in time under the effects of learning, adaptation, stimuli, and so on. Now that chaos theory and fractal geometry have emerged, we expect that fractal boundaries of these psychological regions are the rule, rather than the exception. Following the lead of chaos-theoretic models in medical physiology, we may expect that chaotic attractors and fractal separatrices are important for health. Specifically, we may suggest that thick fractal separatrices in the psyche have an integrating effect. For under the effect of random or chaotic stimuli, the trajectory of the Lewinian model jumps about in small discontinuities, landing in different basins because of the fractal boundaries. This has the effect of integrating the different behaviors of the different attractors into a strongly associated or mixed personality. On the other hand, when the boundaries have become (perhaps in a pathological situation)

too ordered, or *dischaotic*, or if the fractal dimension is too
small, there would be a tendency to manifest one attractor for
some time, until an exceptional stimulus pushes the trajectory
over the edge into the basin of another aspect of the self and
there is a dramatic change in behavior. Posing *dischaos/chaos*
as a binary dichotomy instead of *order/disorder*, we may
call this situation *personality dischaos*, rather than the more
patriarchal *personality disorder*.

Batesonian Application

In a number of papers, Bateson anticipated the fractal
and chaotic models of the psyche. Here, we consider three
examples.

Logical Types

First, consider Bateson's work on logical types and
communication theory (Bateson, 1972, p. 177). Each type may
be viewed, in the Lewinian model, as a region of life space,
a union of basins of several attractors, which enjoys some
isolation from other similar regions. A message is interpreted
by each category, unless it contains an identifier, or address,
specifying one category as its intended destination.

Paradoxes

Next, consider Bateson's analysis of paradox, in which the
meaning of a message in one category denies its meaning in
another category, and vice versa. He likened this situation to
a door buzzer, one of the first models of a negative feedback
oscillator (Bateson, 1979, p. 65). The exemplary paradox
(which is closely related to the double bind, see below) is the

liars paradox ("this sentence is false"), which has recently been shown to generate a chaotic attractor in truth space (Mar & Grim, 1991). We may regard paradox as a fundamentally chaotic process.

The Double Bind

In 1952, with coworker Jay Haley at Stanford University, Bateson developed the double-bind theory of schizophrenia based on his theory of logical types, multiple levels of learning, paradoxes, and communications theory (Bateson, 1972, p. 201). The basic idea of this theory is a cycle involving two people, the dominator and the victim, in which a signal from the dominator is interpreted by the victim on two levels, and each interpretation contradicts the other. See Eglash (1992, chap. 4) for a relevant characterization of mental states in terms of fractal dimension.

In all these examples, an aspect of the individual psyche is divided into multiple levels, a normal structure. But in the pathological situation, a dynamical communication loop is set up between them, like a door buzzer: a disabling oscillation (or chaotic attractor). In our model of the normal psyche based on a dynamical system with fractally intertwined basins (the levels), a small amount of communications noise would be sufficient to stabilize the oscillation. But in a dischaotic psyche, however, the basins are separated by a clean boundary, rather than a sandy beach. Thus, in this model, dischaos is a precondition for schismogenesis, and thus, unwanted oscillations. In this picture a useful property of the psyche might be the *Wada property*: Each point on the boundary of one basin is on the boundary of all (Kennedy & Yorke, 1991). This is known to occur in the dynamical system for the forced damped pendulum. If a psyche has the Wada property, then environmental noise can produce a synthesis of all the levels into a unique self. Alternatively, periodic forcing (turning the pages of a book, for example) may suffice to restore chaos.

Conclusion

These examples should suffice to give an idea what chaos theory can do for the evolution of Lewinian and Batesonian models for the individual or the group psyche. This is as far as a mathematician can go; the next steps are up to the psychologists. By learning a modicum of the mathematical theory of chaotic dynamical systems and their bifurcations, one can develop new theories of dischaotic personality, and therapies too, that can spontaneously pop up. It may be, for example, that electric shocks might be replaced by computer-generated foot massage as a treatment for depression.

In future work we may use the fractal boundary model to suggest some therapies for multiple personality dischaos (MPD), bipolar personality dischaos (BPD), and other dischaos phenomena These would utilize *forces of chaos*, such as chaotic music or exposure to nature, perhaps in a workshop setting. Further, we might try to identify some of the *force of order*, cultural causes, or concomitants of dischaotic personality such as: urbanization, organized religion, patriarchy, monotheism, the Bible, monogamy, marriage, nuclear families, and childrearing practices.

Acknowledgments

It is a pleasure to acknowledge critical discussions with Deena Metzger, Jerry Rasch, and Ray Gwyn Smith and the generosity of Fred Abraham, John Allen, Matt Clinton, Jonathan Cohen, Catherine Heatley, Robert Langs, and

Marsha King in sharing their idea and resources.

CHAPTER A4
CONTROL AND COMMUNICATION

Abstract

Cybernetics is the foundation of this book. The meaning of this word today has evolved in steps from its origins in the work of Norbert Wiener. In this chapter we begin the exegesis of this word with the introduction of his book, *Cybernetics*, written in November of 1947.

Contents

Introduction

As I wrote in the preceding chapter, Norbert Wiener's 1948 book, *Cybernetics, Or Control and Communication in the Animal and the Machine* was one of the first books I read in Ann Arbor.

At that time I had learned little of mathematics. So recently, after a full career in mathematics, I have reread the book, and here I would like to comment on what I now find in it of interest.

Wiener's 1948 Book

The original publication, written in 1947 after the first of the Macy Conferences, comprised an introduction and eight chapters. It is dedicated "To ARTURO ROSENBLEUTH, for many years my companion in science," who died in 1970.

The introduction has 29 pages, and is signed: November, 1947, Instituto de Cardiologia, Ciudad de Mexico. This was the home institution of Rosenblueth. For many years, Wiener spent six moths there, and in alternate years, Rosenblueth spent six months with Wiener at MIT. Rosenblueth is rightfully regarded as one of the founders of cybernetics.

We will return to the introduction later, taking a brief look at the chapters first.

Contents of the 8 Chapters

Wiener assumed a considerable math background of his readers.

1. Newtonian and Bergsonian Time

Here we find a brief and erudite history of science with emphasis on notions of time: meteorology, astronomy of the solar system, paleontology, Darwinian evolution, engineering, automata, neurology, electronics. The essential idea here is Wiener's understanding of the word *machine*.

2. Groups and Statistical Mechanics

This is a short introduction to statistical mechanics, a major branch of modern theoretical physics, and assumes the reader has studied a full undergraduate curriculum of mathematics.

3. Time Series, Information, and Communication

Here Wiener applies statistical mechanics to time series, again, assuming a strong math background. This long chapter includes some of his original mathematical work.

4. Feedback and Oscillation

This is a detailed and somewhat dated mathematical treatment of nonlinear oscillation, with application to neuromuscular tremors, using techniques from the preceding chapters. An alternative for the serious reader might be a recent text on dynamical systems theory.[1]

5. Computing machines and the Nervous System

This is an amazing and prescient description of numerical computing machines, including applications to the computational solution of wave equations, and a forecast of artificial intelligence. This was written at a time when the existing computers were the Eniac, and the Edvac. The Eniac, of 1945, was the first all-electronic computer. The Edvac, the successor to the Eniac, was the first computer to use binary arithmetic and stored programs. In 1947 it was under construction, it was not delivered until 1949.

6. Gestalt and Universals

Here we find a brilliant and probably useful scheme for understanding the recognition of form by the human senses and brain, with many proposed applications for sensory prosthesis. I do not know enough of the subject to assess the comportment of Wiener's proposals of 1947 with the current state of the art.

7. Cybernetics and Psychopathology

Wiener begins,

> It is necessary that I commence this chapter with a disavowal. ... I am not a psychopathologist nor a psychiatrist ...
>
> Nevertheless, the realization that the brain and the computing machine have much in common may suggest new and valid approaches to psychopathology and even to psychiatrics.

This is followed by brief descriptions of half a dozen such approaches.

8. Information, Language, and Society

This short final chapter is quite distinct from the preceding seven. It begins with a discussion of systems, without using the word. Several examples are given which adequately convey the ideas. The terms complex structure, nervous system, organism, and telephone system appear briefly.

In 1947, the year of writing this chapter, Gregory Bateson and Margaret Mead had joined the Macy group, expanding the purview of cybernetics into the social sciences. Also, John von Neumann and Oskar Morgenstern had published their masterpiece on game theory in 1944, of which Wiener was obviously aware.

The concepts of information are introduced in the context of the intercommunications of a social group, hence the title of this chapter.

Wiener expresses some concern for the axioms of the social sciences, especially the assumption of homeostasis in several contexts.

Wiener's Introduction

Written in November, 1947, this section of the book is probably the last to be written. Also, it is the longest, other than Chapter 3. The word cybernetics occurs about nine times in the introduction, while in the eight chapters it is hardly mentioned. The topics presented are:

- The role of Arturo Rosenblueth in the development of cybernetics.
- The role of World War 2 in the choice of topics.
- Wiener's contributions to the development of the electronic computing machine.
- The importance of feedback in problems of control.
- Control of anti-aircraft guns.
- Information, entropy, and error-correction of communications.
- Choice of the name *cybernetics* for the emerging field combining control and communication theory in the summer of 1947.
- Credits for the roles played by Alan Turing, Walter Pitts, Warren McCulloch, John von Neumann, and the Macy Foundation.
- A complete history of cybernetics.
- Doubts that cybernetics might contribute to the solution of the diseases of society.
- Hopes it might contribute to the fields of prosthesis for lost limbs, and artificial intelligence for automatic factories.

Wiener ends his introduction with this fear:

Those of us who have contributed to the new science of cybernetics thus stand in a moral position which is, to say the least, not very comfortable. We have contributed to the initiation of a new science which, as I have said, embraces technical developments with great possibilities for good and for evil.

Conclusion: What is Cybernetics?

We are left, at the end of 165 pages, a bit unsure of the full meaning of the word *cybernetics*, as of November, 1947. It is only later that the addition of the general systems theory of von Bertalanffy (1937), the self-organization theory of Ross Ashby (1947), and the system dynamics of Jay Forrester (1970) established cybernetics as we know it today.[2]

Notes

1   See, for example, (Strogatz, 1994) or (Garfinkel, 2017).
2   See (Capra and Luisi, 2014; Part 2).

Chapter A5
Five Legacies of David Loye:

Abstract

My personal memories of David Loye, Riane Eisler, Ervin Laszlo, and the General Evolution Research Group (GERG) during our partnership of 36 years. The five legacies discussed are GERG, Partnership, Chaos, Darwin, and Action Research

Publication

An earlier version, written in March 2022, was published in the *Journal of Partnership Studies*.

Contents

0. Introduction

David Loye was hard at work on new book projects when he passed. What he had already achieved was enormous, and I will comment here on his work during the time I knew him, from mid-1985 up through mid 2021. These were years of friendship and collaboration of great value to me. He exerted crucial influence on my work. Here are some of the highlights, seen through my mathematical lens.

One of Dave's many books, *The Evolutionary Outrider*, an edited collection from 1998, is the primary source for this memoir. Four of its chapters are especially relevant here, three by David, and one by Riane Eisler. I also contributed a chapter on the social significance of the World Wide Web.

1. Before GERG, 1960-1980

In the 1960s, I had decided that my mathematical work must be useful in regard to world problems. This was in the ambiance of the Cold War, ongoing since 1947. In the 1970s I began my focus on computational studies of chaotic dynamical systems. I embraced catastrophe theory because of its broad applicability in the sciences. In 1980, I tried to work with research groups in the biological sciences but suffered disappointments stemming from complications of large grants. I temporarily gave up my focus on world problems.

2. Meeting Riane, David, and Ervin, 1985

Then, in 1985, I received a phone call out of the blue. It was Dave Loye, a social scientist living nearby in Carmel. He said that Ervin Laszlo was visiting from Italy and would like to meet me. I was teaching full time then, so we agreed that they would drive to Santa Cruz for a short meeting. He soon arrived with his partner, Riane Eisler, and Laszlo. We had lunch and talked for a long time.

It appeared that they had a major project in mind in connection with world problems, and I was intrigued. Maybe it was too early to give up on my desire to do useful math. I had not tried working with social scientists, so I signed on. Doing good was back on the table. I soon learned that Ervin had been involved in the Club of Rome (famous for the *Limits to Growth* book of 1971) in the 1970s, The Club of Rome was part of the stimulus for the new project.

This new project involved the assembly of a group of scholars in many disciplines to generate ideas for the future of mankind. Cultural evolution was a central theme. First steps were already underway following a meeting in Budapest in 1984.[1]

3. Beginning of GERG, 1986

Our meeting in Santa Cruz resulted in my invitation to a further meeting of the new group at the Salk Institute in La Jolla, hosted by Jonas Salk himself, in March of 1986. Besides David, Riane, Ervin, and myself, John Corliss and several others attended. The main outcome of this event was the adoption by the group of the name *General Evolution Research Group*, or *GERG*, and the founding of our journal, *World Futures: The Journal of General Evolution*, with Ervin as editor.

The Salk meeting of 1986 was followed by a series of further meetings, in Florence, Bologna, Prague, and other European cities, during which the size of the group grew substantially. The journal also thrived, and I published several articles there, from 1990 through 2011.

The genesis of GERG was recounted by David in Chapter 3

of *The Evolutionary Outrider*.

4. Partnership Studies, 1987

One of our ideas for GERG was a series of books, the first of which, was Riane's masterwork, *The Chalice and the Blade: Our History, Our Future*, which founded Partnership Studies as a field in 1987. This carried, on the copyright page, the inscription: *A Catalyst Book of the General Evolution Research Group and the Center for Partnership Studies.* I inscribed a similar reference to GERG in my book, *Chaos, Gaia, Eros* in 1988.

The two themes of *The Chalice and the Blade*, Partnership Studies and Cultural Transformation Theory, have been developed extensively by Riane, but David's creativity was manifest in both.

4.1 Partnership and dominator models

Quoting from Riane's Introduction:

> One result of re-examining human society from a gender-holistic perspective has been a new theory of cultural evolution. This theory, which I have called cultural transformation theory, proposed that underlying the great surface diversity of human culture are two basic models of society.
>
> The first, which I call the *dominator* model, is what is popularly termed either patriarchy or matriarchy — the ranking of one half of humanity over the other. The second, in which social relations are primarily based on the principle of *linking* rather than ranking, may best be described as the *partner-*

ship model.[2]

4.2 Cultural transformation theory (CTT)

Quoting again from the Introduction:

> Cultural transformation theory further proposes
> that the original direction in the mainstream of our
> cultural evolution was toward partnership but that,
> following a period of chaos and almost total cultur-
> al disruption, there occurred a fundamental social
> shift ... from a partnership to a dominator model ... [3]

These two themes remained central to David's thinking throughout his career.

5. *Chaos Theory, 1991*

Chaos theory studies mathematical objects called *chaotic attractors* and *bifurcations*. The latter have many important applications to the social sciences which now abound in the literature of this society. One of these applications is fundamental to CTT, as indicated above.

Another pillar in David's evolution followed from the chaos revolution of the 1960s and 1970s. News of this development in the mathematics of dynamical systems came indirectly from me, by way of my brother Fred.[4] Together, psychologists David, Fred, and Allan Combs founded the *Society for Chaos Theory in Psychology and Life Sciences (SCTPLS)* in 1991 to further the applications of chaos theory.

6. The Darwin Project, 1994

Sometime around 1994 David discovered the second half of Darwin's theory of evolution, and this became one of his main preoccupations. In a series of books he excavated Darwin's lost theory, which had been buried by Darwin's heirs.[5] The first half, based on the crucial idea of the *survival of the fittest*, became the dogma of evolution theory over the years. Meanwhile the lost second half, based on the crucial idea of *love*, championed the evolution of the *moral sense*. David felt that exhuming Darwin's theory of love could help save the world, and thus, fit the overall program of GERG. To further this project, he founded the *Darwin Project*, which I joined many years ago.

7. Action Research, 1998

Another central theme of David's work — related to GERG, partnership, chaos, and Darwin — was his expanded version of the action research idea of Kurt Lewin of 1951.[6]

7.1 Kurt Lewin

Lewin was born Jewish in Poland, earned a PhD in Gestalt psychology in Berlin during World War 1, and moved to the USA in 1933. He founded two major action research institutes, the Commission on Community Relations of the American Jewish Congress in 1968 and the Research Center for Group Psychology at MIT in 1945. He is remembered as one of the founding fathers of social psychology and social engineering.

Around 1970 I became interested in Lewin's seminal work on topographical psychology. Dynamical systems theory was in a crisis, and I was searching for applications from which I might find a new direction for my future research. Lewin had suggested that psychological dynamics was guided by a vectorfield on a behavior space, under which stable behaviors were represented by attractors of the vectorfield.

In addition to his field theory, Lewin introduced the concept of action research in 1944, after some 10 years of development. He presented it in an article in 1946, and in his book *Resolving Social Conflicts* of 1948.

Lewin reacted to his life experience of anti-Semitism — including the death of his mother in a Nazi gas chamber and his escape from Hitler in 1933 — with a special interest in racism and minority relations. He participated in a 1946 workshop for the Connecticut Interracial Commission. It was in the context of his field work in Connecticut that he honed the action research idea into an effective method of social work, and remedy for racism.

Action research, like all scientific research, involves repetition of the hermeneutic cycle: modeling, testing, model revision, more testing, and so on. This aspect of Lewin's work had a great effect on my own work. In fact, in my book *Chaos, Gaia, Eros*, written in 1988, I wrote:

Lewin's contact with the hermeneutical tradition of Dilthey in Berlin led to his development of social psychology and action research, which branched from hermeneutics, courageously carrying out the hermeneutic program in the practical context of social psychology.[7]

7.2 David Loye

After our meeting, David gave me a signed copy of his book, *The Healing of a Nation*. The inscription is dated

November 21, 1985. The book was honored by the Anisfield-Wolfe Book Award for best scholarly book on race relations. It was dedicated to the memory of Kurt Lewin and W. E. B. Du Bois.

The book is divided into two parts — *Part One: The Years of Sickness and the Search for Therapies*, and *Part Two: Healing the Nation*. The latter comprises six chapters of remedies, two devoted to Kurt Lewin. These two amount to about ten percent of the entire book, and remain the best source I know for Lewin's life and ideas. They are the main resource for this section, along with David's chapter 12 in *The Evolutionary Outrider*, entitled *Evolutionary Action Theory: a Brief Outline*.

David was obviously aware of Lewin's action research and its applications early in his career. But by 1998 he had significantly extended the idea, and it played an important role in all his thinking. The terms *active human agent, evolutionary action theory, active moral agent,* and *moral action* appear throughout his work. His presentation of this extended theory comprises Chapter 12 of *The Evolutionary Outrider*. Therein he wrote:

> In psychology, the action-research approach coupled with the field theory of Kurt Lewin remains the most advanced statement of the perspective of action-oriented theory. In evolutionary theory, general evolution theorist Ervin Laszlo is the pioneering exponent of this perspective.[8]

David's extension of action research involves the second half of Darwin's legacy: Moral sensitivity exerts an influence on evolution by determining which options to promote by human activity. Ervin Laszlo's book of 1987, *Evolution, the Grand Synthesis*, is a brilliant development of this idea in the context of a complete history of evolutionary systems thinking from the Greeks forward.

8. After GERG, 2000

Due to the proximity of Carmel to Santa Cruz, my personal relationship with Riane and David developed into a lasting and supportive friendship. As time went on, the vitality of GERG diminished. Riane was primarily occupied with her very successful Center for Partnership Studies, its journal, and many important lectures worldwide. Meanwhile, David settled into his major focus on Darwin's second half, the related Darwin Project, and his series of books on Darwin beginning in 2007. And I continued my applications of chaos theory in various fields.

9. Conclusion

Collecting the key events of this story into a chronological list, we have:

1984, Ervin's pre-GERG meeting in Budapest
1985, My meeting with David, Riane, and Ervin
1986, Group meeting with Jonas Salk, founding of
      GERG and *World Futures*
1987, Riane's *The Chalice and the Blade,*
      Ervin's Evolution, the Grand Synthesis
1988, Writing of my book, *Chaos, Gaia, Eros*
1991, Creation of the *Society for Chaos Theory and*
      the Life Sciences
1992, David's first publication on the moral sense
1994, Beginning of David's *Darwin Project*
1998, David's *The Evolutionary Outrider*
2007, David's first book on Darwin's lost theory

David's career spanned an enormous spectrum of the social sciences, systems thinking, and integrative studies. His creativity was spectacular, his influence enduring. He was the epitome of partnership, cooperation, action research, and human-action. He performed his teachings, walking the talk, leaping over boundaries.

Notes

1   For the full story by David Loye, see (Loye, 1998; ch. 3), and also the website, thedarwinproject.com.
2   (Eisler, 1987; p. xvii)
3   (Eisler, 1987; p. xvii)
4   (F. D. Abraham, 1990)
5   See especially (Loye, 2007).
6   See (Loye, 1988; p. 8, and ch. 12).
7   (Abraham, 1994; pp. 16-17.
8   (Loye, 1998; p. 170)

CHAPTER A6
THE LINDISFARNE DREAM

Abstract

The Lindisfarne Association, created by William Irwin Thompson in the 1970s, was a wonderful attempt to influence the future of world cultural history. It had a great influence on me in the 1980s and beyond.

Contents

Introduction

Among the philosophic organizations seeking to change the evolution of world cultural history, one of the most ambitious was the Lindisfarne Association, created by the late William Irwin Thompson.

Bill Thompson

Bill Thompson was a poet, cultural historian, and activist. Once professor at MIT, he dropped out of academia in 1972 and began the Lindisfarne adventure as a residential community on Long Island. He also published more than two dozen influential books, including:

- *At the Edge of History: Speculations on the Transformation of Culture*, 1971.
- *Passages about Earth: An Exploration of the New Planetary Culture*, 1974.
- *The Time Falling Bodies Take to Light: Mythology, Sexuality and the Origins of Culture*, 1981.
- *Pacific Shift*, 1986,
- *Imaginary Landscape: Making Worlds of Myth and Science*, 1989,
- *Transforming History: A Curriculum for Cultural Evolution*, 2001.
- *Thinking Together at the Edge of History: A Memoire of the Lindisfarne Association, 1972-2012*, 2016.

Andra Akers

The late Andra Akers was an actress on stage and screen in the 1970s and 80s. Upon retiring in 1986 she founded the

International Synergy Institute to seek solutions to world problems. I met her at a conference at the Ojai Foundation called The Way of the Warrior in May, 1984, while she was acting in the film, Desert Hearts. She arranged a lecture for me at the American Film Institute in 1986, and there I met Bill Thompson. He kindly agreed to read an early draft of my book, *Chaos, Gaia, Eros*, and made several helpful suggestions. In October, 1988, he invited me to a meeting of the Lindisfarne Association at the Esalen Institute, where I became a member of the Group. Andra Akers was active in the Lindisfarne Association until her premature passing in 2002.

Joint Works

In the subsequent years Bill and I worked on projects together — acknowledged in Bill's book, *Imaginary Landscape*, 1989 — and published occasional reports, such as :

The electronic rose window, 1993,
Of Angels, extraterrestrials, lost continents, and other strange attractors, 1993,
The geometry of angels, 1998.

Courtney Sale Ross

As a result of a review of my book, *Chaos, Gaia, Eros*, by Allan Badiner appearing in the Yoga Journal in 1994, I met Courtney Sale Ross, the founder of the Ross School in East Hampton, NY. Bill and I worked together with Courtney 1995-2015 to create a curriculum for the school, with Bill as the primary author. This is presented in full detail in Bill's book, *Transforming History*, 2001.

My main contribution to this joint work was to include the fundamental concepts of my own mathematical specialty, complex dynamical systems theory, aka chaos theory. Such ideas as attractors, basins, and bifurcations abound. The application of these ideas to history and the social sciences was pioneered by the mathematicians René Thom and Christopher Zeeman in 1970s, and comprise the core of my book, *Chaos, Gaia, Eros*, published in 1994. This subject is treated further in later chapters of this book.

Conclusion

My working relationship with Bill continued until his passing in 2020. My later works will be impoverished for lack of his generous feedback and encouragement. Most especially this book, which is an effort in the spirit of the Lindisfarne mission, desperately needed his participation.

PART B
AMERICA TODAY

CHAPTER B1
A DYNAMICS LEXICON

Abstract

This is an optional excursion into the jargon of chaos theory.

Contents

Dynamical systems theory is a new branch of mathematics about a century old. It has great power in modeling complex natural systems. Two aspects of special importance are bifurcations and chaos, as indicated by the title of the periodical: *International Journal of Bifurcation and Chaos.* Here is a concise lexicon of the mathematical jargon of this new field.

Systems

System is a word with multiple meanings. We try to avoid using it without a modifier, for example, nervous system, or economic system.

Dynamical systems

A continuous *dynamical system* is a mathematical model for a flow in a geometric space. Each point in the space flows along a curve called a *trajectory*. Each trajectory ends up in a terminal set of points in the space called an *attractor*. Many trajectories may tend to the same attractor. The set of all points tending to the same attractor is called its *basin*.[1]

Dynamical Schemes

When a dynamical system is changed by control parameters, the configuration of attractors and basins may remarkably change. The system comprising an dynamical system with control parameters, and specification of the space of these parameters, is a *dynamical scheme*.

Bifurcations

When a dynamical scheme is changed by a parameter, the configuration of attractors and basins may remarkably change. These events are called *bifurcations.* They are classified in three categories: *subtle, explosive, and catastrophic.* Catastrophic biurcations are also known as *catastrophes.*

Catastrophe Theory

Catastrophe theory is a derivative of dynamical systems theory created by René Thom since 1966.[2] It provides explicit models for some of the simplest catastrophies. Many applications of Thom's ideas were developed by Christopher Zeeman in the 1970s.

Chaos theory is a popular name for the applied and computational aspects of dynamical systems theory, developed since 1974.

The basic ideas of these theories — attractors, basins, and bifurcations — have been extensively applied in the sciences, history, and philosophy.

Catastrophe is the underlying mathematical idea of many of my writings. This concept is also known by other names, such as saltatory leap, major transformation, morphogenesis, or schismogenesis.

Notes

1   For more details, see (Abraham, 2016.)

Chapter B2
Schismogenesis Today

Abstract

Here are some exemplary cases of schismogenesis from recent history, 1960 to 2021.

Contents

1. Introduction

We now consider some examples of schismogenesis, paradigm shift, bifurcation, or catastrophe. These terms are not quite synonyms, and are closely related.

Bifurcation is a mathematical terms for a significant change in the portrait of a *dynamical scheme*, that is, a dynamical system depending on parameters. These occur in three categories: subtle, explosive, and catastrophic. A catastrophic bifurcation is also called a *catastrophe*.

Paradigm shift refers to a bifurcation in a dynamical scheme modeling a set of ideas or mental states.

Schismogenesis and *major cultural transformation* refer to a bifurcation in a dynamical scheme modeling part of world cultural history with historical time as the parameter.

Ignoring context, we may use the term *bifurcation* for all these cases, whether mathematical, mental, or historical. And *bifurcation* may ambiguously refer either to the mathematical model, or the historical situation which is the target of the model.

2. Bifurcations, 25,000 BCE to 1960 CE

Major cultural transformation is the subject of my earlier book, *Chaos, Gaia, Eros*. When I sent the manuscript to my editor in 1988, John Brockman, he said it was a chaotic book. He secured a contract for it with Harper, and it sat on various editorial desks for six years. It was finally published in 1994. The editors kept asking me, what is the book about? My answer was there in the Introduction. And here is a summary.

Three gods or principles ruled from prehistoric times, 25,000 BCE or so. In Ancient Greece they were called *Chaos, Gaia*, and *Eros*, the Orphic trinity. That book tells the story of the *long line of Plato* in epochs:

(0) Prehistory was chaotic until 10,000 BCE. This phase is the original *Chaotic Epoch*, associated with the Orphic god *Chaos*.

(1) The agricultural revolution inaugurated a new phase 10,000 to 4,000 BCE, the *Static Epoch*, associated with the Orphic god *Gaia*.

(2) Then the invention of the wheel triggered another phase, the *Periodic Epoch*, 4,000 BCE to 1960. Associated with the Orphic god *Eros*, it ushered in cities and writing. This includes the Axial Age, 800-300 BCE, described by Karl Jaspers in 1949.

(3) And then, around 1960, the original Chaotic phase was revived by the Chaos Revolution in mathematics and the sciences, starting another cycle of the great wheel of world cultural history. We are now in this new Chaotic Epoch.

This was the portrait of the long line of Plato up to 1988, the time of writing of *Chaos, Gaia, Eros*. Now we may update that portrait from 1960 to 2021. This period of 62 years is full of transformations, comprising a complex of schismogeneses.

And now we arrive at some cultural bifurcations from this period.

3. Bifurcations, 1960 to 2021

It appears that we are in a major cultural transformation at present. It has been evolving since the Chaos Revolution of the 1960s. Unlike the arrivals of agriculture and the wheel, this process of schismogenesis has unrolled within my lifetime.

After recalling the exemplary case of plate tectonics, I will recount my personal view of the bifurcation process in the context of American history. These are some of the threads: Racism, LGBTQ, Women, Drugs, Environment, CoViD-19,

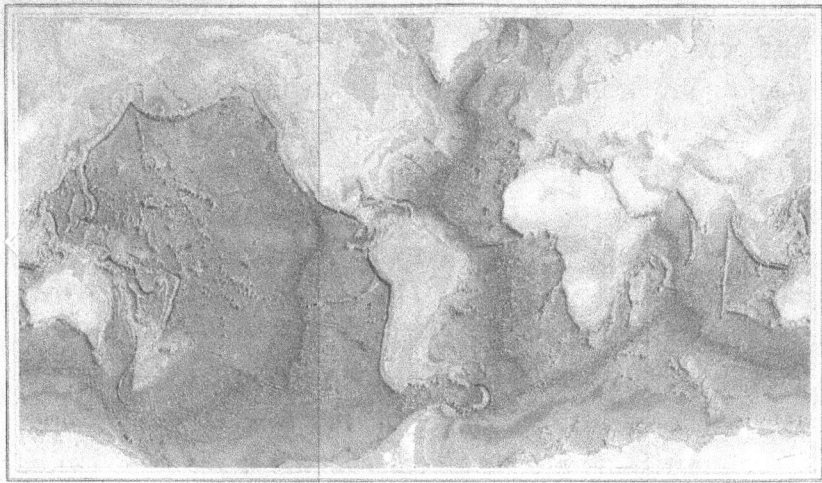

Figure 1. Continents and mid-ocean ridges. From the Wikipedia entry on Marie Tharp, pioneer of mapping the ocean floor. The continents drifted away from the ridges.

and Politics.

3.1. Plate tectonics, 1965 to 1967

The discovery of plate tectonics is an excellent example of schismogenesis in the context of the history and sociology of science, as analyzed by Ludwik Fleck and Thomas Kuhn.[1] Plate tectonics is a theory of the motion of tectonic plates, the giant pieces making up the lithosphere (crust) of the Earth, and accounting for the phenomenon of continental drift.[2]

Cartography has been evolving since Babylonian maps of the world, around 2300 BCE. One of the first accurate maps of the entire world was published by Gerardus Mercator in 1569. And already in this map, it may be seen that the outlines of the continents could be fit together, into a conjectured original land mass. This was noticed in 1596 by Abraham Ortelius, the creator of the first world atlas. He suggested that the Americas were torn away from Europe and Africa by earthquakes and floods. The original land mass was named *Pangea* by Alfred Wegener in 1912. Apparently this super-continent bifurcated repeatedly, and the fragments shifted about in a process Wegener called *continental drift*.

His theory was generally rejected in the first half of the 20th century. It evolved into the theory of plate tectonics with the proposal of Arthur Holmes in 1920 that the lithosphere was composed of separate pieces, called *tectonic plates*, with junctions beneath the seas. In 1958, S. W. Carey proposed that movements of the plates carried the continents along. The discovery of mid-ocean ridges and seafloor spreading, as supported by the work of Marie Tharp, led to the Plate Tectonics Revolution of 1965-67, that is, the acceptance of Wegener's plate tectonics theory.

This revolution was a paradigm shift in the sense of Fleck and Kuhn.[3] The gradual accumulation of evidence reached a tipping point, and a major transformation, a catastrophe, occurred in the history of science. Ironically, the paradigm shift concerned bifurcations (fractures, or schisms) in the Earth's crust. The remaining examples are all more recent.

3.2 Racism (Black Lives Matter)

This thread in American history goes back to slavery in the early days of the country. This officially ended with the American Civil War, 1861 to 1965, but racial prejudice against Blacks continues to the present day. Legal and voting rights were established in the 14th Amendment (1868) and 15th Amendment (1870).

In the 1960s, there was a major popular movement for Civil Rights, in which the Reverend Martin Luther King Jr., was a pivotal figure. Despite some significant improvements, racial prejudice remained.

In this year, 2020, the Black Lives Matter movement gained widespread support among Americans. It seems that a major cultural transformation is underway.

3.3 Women (Abortion)

In *Chaos, Gaia, Eros*, the transformation from gylany to patriarchy was identified with the bifurcation from Chaos to Gaia, from the Chaotic Epoch to the Static.[4] In American history, this was manifest in unequal rights for women. The Women's Suffrage movement, begun around 1848, resulted in the voting rights for women in the 19th Amendment (1920). Even so, unequal rights persisted in the home, at work, in sexual relations, and throughout society. In the 1970s, following the progress of civil rights for Black Americans, women fought and won rights for abortion in the Roe v. Wade ruling of 1973, and made progress toward equal pay and other rights.

In 2020, the MeToo movement won major cases against men accused of sexual violence. In 2021 and 2022, the government of Texas enacted draconian anti-abortion legislation. Again, it seems like a major cultural transformation is underway.

3.4 LGBTQ (Gay Marriage)

Lesbian, Gay, Bisexual, Transgender, and Queer rights, also with a long history, showed a sharp advance since the 1960s. There was a major breakthrough in a landmark Supreme

Court case of 1967. This was the civil rights case, which
liberated LGBTQ rights as a side effect. Same-sex marriage
was legalized, state-by-state, from 2004 to 2015.

3.5 Drugs (Psychedelics)

Psychoactive drugs — alcohol, tobacco, opium, cocaine,
and the psychedelics — in popular use for thousands of years,
have been prohibited by law in the USA and around the world
in modern times.[5]

Opium has been controlled since 1912. In the USA, alcohol
was prohibited by the 18th Amendment to the Constitution in
1920, and ended in 1933 by the 21st Amendment. Cannabis
regulation began in 1937.

Psychedelics have been prohibited as well — LSD since
1968, and psilocybin, mescaline, and DMT since 1971,
in connection with Nixon's War on Drugs. Beginning in
2018, this regulation has declined. Psychedelic research has
been resumed, and cannabis legalization in the USA is now
progressing state-by-state as I write.

Despite legal restrictions, the psychedelic revolution was a
crucial element in the development of Hip culture in the 1960s
and 1970s. It is ongoing today.

3.6 Environment (Global Warming)

Concern for the environmental impacts of the burgeoning
human population and its industries must have been common
for generations, but I became aware only in the 1960s. Here
are just a few highlights of this epic schismogenesis:

- 1961. Rachel Carson's book, *Silent Spring*, 1961, was
  hugely popular and influential.[6] Toxic pesticides

and weed killers, especially DDT, were killing birds. Concerns for the pollution of top soil, the atmosphere, and the oceans spawned the environmental movement.

- 1966. After an LSD trip, Stewart Brand created the *Whole Earth Catalog*. This had a huge influence on the development of the environmental movement among young people in the early Hip culture. He was also instrumental in creating the Trips Festival of 1966, in which the Grateful Dead were launched in the rock-and-roll revolution.
- 1967. The Zero Population Growth (ZPG) movement was cofounded by Stanford University professor Paul Ehrlich. It morphed into the Population Connection, which survives today.
- 1968. The book *The Population Bomb* by Paul and Anne Ehrlich was a best-seller. It featured a pessimistic forecast of the effects of the human population explosion.[7]
- 1968. The Club of Rome was founded in Italy to mitigate the deleterious effects of the explosive growth of population and consumerism on the biosphere.
- 1970. *Mother Earth News* provided a bible for a movement back to the farm.
- 1970. The Club of Rome supported Jay W. Forrester of MIT, the founder of System Dynamics, to create World1, a model of the whole Earth's social and economic systems in competition with limited natural resources.
- 1971. The book *World Dynamics* reported on the technology of the World1 simulation.
- 1972. The book *The Limits of Growth* published extensive graphics from World1 showing the disaster that was predicted if population were not limited.

- 1973. The Lindisfarne Association was founded by world cultural historian William Irwin Thompson. He collected a group of intellectuals to imagine ways to save the planet, including ways to create a truly post-industrial green civilization. Among the members were E. F. Schumacher, Hazel Henderson, Gregory Bateson, Stewart Brand, Francisco Varela, Marshall McLuhan, Michael Murphy, Richard Baker-roshi, David Spangler, James Lovelock, and many others, including myself.
- 1973. The Endangered Species Act was passed by the US Congress.
- 1984. *The State of the World* book series appeared, aimed at Environmental Sustainability, Climate Change, the Global Food Crisis, Education for Sustainability, and so on.

All these concerns are ongoing today. After a decline for a decade or two, a massive revival of environmental concern has spawned widespread activism.

3.7 CoVid-19 (The 1st Big Lie)

The CoViD-19 pandemic raging since January 2020, especially out of control in the USA, is not an example of schismogenesis. In the fight against the coronavirus pandemic, progressives consent to wear masks, keep social distance, and accept vaccination, while conservatives flout the rules. This is an example of schismogenesis, ongoing as I write.

This schism was created by the first of the then-president's two big lies: He insisted from the beginning of CoViD-19 that there was no pandemic, that masks were ineffective, that vaccines would not work, and that there were simple cures such as kitchen bleach. The disagreement over the benefits and risks of vaccination, in particular, amounts almost to a civil war. The anti-vaxxers threaten violence to escape vaccination and mask mandates.

3.8 Politics (The 2nd Big Lie)

In the USA, the conservative group is roughly identical to the Republican party, while the progressives are Democrats. Thus, the growing split extends to issues such as guns, vaccinations, animal rights, health care, taxation, immigration, support for democracy, and all the rest. While the Democratic Party is roughly stable on the progressive axis, the Republican Party has moved rapidly to the right. It seems now actually anti-democratic. The central issue is Trump's Second Big Lie, insisting that the 2020 presidential election was fraudulent. It seems that almost all Republicans in Congress, and nearly no Democrats, support it.

4. Summary (Alignment)

These are some of the events that have energized and accelerated schismogeneses since 1960 — the development of divisions of global society into two groups, for and against the momentum of change on all these fronts: racism, women, gays, drugs, the environment, CoViD-19 mitigations, the Election Big Lie, democracy, and so on.

Strangely, there is an alignment along the scale of the conservative versus progressive axis in each case. Progressives promoting change on all fronts, and conservatives aligned against all of them.

Each of these cultural bifurcations may be modeled with the fold catastrophe of Thom's theory, as in Zeeman's applications to social processes described in the first chapter (and later chapters) of this book.

The first three epochs described in *Chaos, Gaia, Eros* are of great length:

0. Original Chaotic/Chaos, 15,000 years
1. Static/Gaia, 6,000 years
2. Periodic/Eros, 6,000 years

Yet our current epoch has hardly begun:

3. New Chaotic/Chaos, 60 years and ongoing.

Actual bifurcations in cultural history are complex events, with numerous transformations, large and small, extending over substantial periods of time. The chaos revival begun around 1960 is still underway.

Like aftershocks of a large earthquake, we are now rumbling in the aftermath of the 1960s. The psychedelic revolution may be the primary trigger, the original earthquake for our current events.

Notes

1   (Fleck, 1935), (Kuhn, 1962)
2   Wikipedia has an excellent account of this subject under Plate Tectonics.
3   See Chapter 1 for the story of paradigm shift.
4   See (Eisler, 1987) for the theory of prehistoric gylany.
5   For a comprehensive history of drugs, see (Breen, 2019).
6   (Carson, 1961)
7   (Ehrlich, 1968)

Chapter B3
The Madness of Crowds

Abstract

The madness of crowds, is a classical topic for social philosophy and cultural history. An early work by Charles MacKay (1841) defined the thread. Following World War 2, works by Hannah Arendt (1951) and Elias Canetti (1960) revived the subject. A recent work by William Bernstein (2021) updates it with a summary of relevant social psychology research. In this chapter, we extract from Canetti and Bernstein some aspects of the subject useful for our modeling project.

Contents

Preface

Our subject is known varoiously as mass insanity, mass mania, madness of crowds, madness of groups, delusions of crowds, and popular delusions. Among these synonyms my favorite is madness of crowds. There is a long thread of literature on this topic, and recently, a growing body of scientific publication. For our mathematical model of madness, we will make use of this scientific literature. A clarification of the word *crowd* is provided by the book *Crowds and Power* by Elias Canetti (1960).

Firtly, he defines a *pack* as a small horde of ten or twelve people. It is a band which cannot grow. Of packs there are four types: hunting pack, war pack, lamenting pack, and increase pack. An increase pack may transform into a crowd crystal, which then grows into a crowd.

> The crowd, suddenly there where there was nothing before, is a mysterious and universal phe-nomenon. A few people may have been standing together — five, ten or twelve, not more; nothing has been announced, nothing is expected. Suddenly everywhere is black with people and more come streaming from all sides as though streets have only one direction. Most of them do not know what has happened and, if questioned, have no answer; but they hurry to be there where most other people are. There is a determination in their movement which is quite different from the expression of ordinary curiosity. It seems as though the movement of some of them transmits itself to the others. But that is not all; they have a goal which is there before they can find words for it. This goal is the blackest spot

where most people are gathered.

This is the extreme form of the spontaneous crowd … [1]

Canetti wrote before the advent of the internet. The contemporary version of this phenomenon is a post on social media going viral.

A Chronology of Madness

Here I am abstracting from two long books, *Memoirs of Extraordinary Popular Delusions and the Madness of Crowds*, by Charles MacKay, 1841, and *The Delusions of Crowds* by William J. Bernstein, 2021.

Charles MacKay, 1841

MacKay (1814-1849) was a popular poet and editor. His book is an excruciatingly detailed account of selected exemplary cases. They concern religious, financial, and various other manias. Here is a list of his 16 chapters, rearranged in chronological order.

Ch. 8. Influences of Politics and Religion on the Hair and Beard, 1 CE
Ch. 15. Duels and Ordeals, 501
Ch. 9. The Crusades, 700
Ch. 4. Alchymists, 730
Ch. 5, Modern Prophesies, 950
Ch. 16. Relics, 11th C.
Ch. 14. Popular Admiration of Great Thieves, 13th C
Ch. 10. Witch Mania, 1234
Ch. 12. Haunted Houses, 1259

Ch. 6. Fortune-Telling, 1500
Ch. 11. Slow Poisoners, 1613
Ch. 7. Magnetizers, 1625
Ch. 2. South-Sea Bubble, 1711
Ch. 1. Mississippi Scheme, 1719-20
Ch. 13. Popular Folies of Great Cities, 1787

We may sort these into the three categories: financial mania, religious madness, and other.

Financial manias involving delusions of instant wealth:
Ch. 3. Tulipomania, 1634
Ch. 2. South-Sea Bubble, 1711
Ch. 1. Mississippi Scheme, 1719-20

Religious manias involving eschatology (concerning the final destiny of the soul and of humankind), Armageddon (where the final battle will be fought between the forces of good and evil), and end-times (the end of the Universe, or coming of a messiah):
Ch. 5. Modern Prophesies, 950

Other manias involving various themes.

We are especialy interested in religious mania due its relevance to our main interest, the mathematics of civil division and civil war. MacKay's single chapter in this category begins with an important example:

An epidemic terror of the end of the world has several times spread over the nations. The most remarkable was that which seized Christendom about the middle of the tenth century. Numbers of fanatics appeared in France, Germany, and Italy at that time, preaching that the thousand years prophesied in the Apocalypse as the term of the world's duration were about to expire, and that the Son of Man would appear in the clouds to judge the godly and the ungodly.

Among the near synonyms — Armageddon, Messiah, Second Coming, etc — we will usually choose *end-times* as a convenient representative.

William Bernstein, 2021

Bernstein is a neurologist, financial theorist, and historian. Recapitulating some of MacKay's exemplars, he adds further examples from the recent two centuries. In addition, there is a unique and valuable analysis of the mechanisms common to many popular manias, drawn from the recent literature of experimental psychology and the neurosciences.

Bernstein's first three chapters overlap the time frame of MacKay's book of 1841. Ch. 3 recapitulates Ch. 2 of MacKay. The remaining chapters postdate Mackay. They fit into the three categories (financial mania, religious mania, and other) with 8 chapters in our main category of interest, religious mania. Here is a list of these chapters, with brief synopses.

Ch. 1. Joachim's Children
(German Peasant's War, 1525)

This chapter is named for Joachim of Fiore (1135-1202) who was known for, among many other things, his vision of the end-times forecast in three books of the bible: Ezekiel, Daniel, and Revelation. Joachim predicted three ages of Man before the Apocalypse: the Age of the Father, the Age of the Son, and the Age of the Holy Spirit. This final epoch was to begin in 1260. Bernstein calls the historical followers of this theory, *Joachim's children*.

The first child of Joachim, or madness, described at length in this chapter, is the German Peasant's War of 1525.

In the early sixteenth century, poor crops, a rapacious aristocracy, and Lutheran zeal combined to ignite bloody popular revolt. Legend has it that on June 23, 1523, six years after Luther nailed his ninety-six theses to the door of the Wittenberg Castle Church, the countess of Lupfen-Stühlengen in Swabia, just north of central Switzerland, ordered twelve hundred peasants intent on harvesting their hay to instead collect snail shells on which to mount her presumably large supply of thread. The countess's acute need for these shells so angered her peasants that it triggered an uprising that spread across much of German-speaking Europe over the following two years.

In 1524-1525, peasant armies fought a series of battles, collectively known as the German Peasants' War (colloquially, the *War of Snails*), against *landknechts*, mercenaries hired by the local aristocrats. These encounters more often than not resulted in the wholesale slaughter of approximately one hundred thousand of the poorly trained and armed rebels.

Throughout most of this episode, social, and not religious, concerns drove the German rebels, loosely known as the Schwabian League, but the revolt's bloody denouement was largely the work of

a millennialist priest named Thomas Müntzer and
his deluded, frenzied followers.[2]

Müntzer and his followers are children of Joachim, in
that Müntzer had read and interpreted Joachim. He gave
inflammatory millennialist sermons, claiming that God had
chosen him to bring about the Apocalypse. He encouraged
7000 rebels to rush toward the mercenaries. Most were killed.
Müntzer himself was captured and beheaded.

Ch. 2. Believers and Rogues
(Anabaptist Madness, 1533-1535)

Anabaptism, a new Protestant sect, emerged in Münster
in 1534, less than a decade after the War of Snails. It was
characterized by several heresies, especially, baptism of adults,
rather than babies. It evolved into mad episodes in Germany
and Holland, the Anabaptist Madness, 1533-1535.

The first such episode was triggered by Melchior Hoffman,
who spewed reformist heresies from 1523. He took the Book
of Revelation seriously, and preached an immanent apocalypse
in 1533. He was imprisoned by the authorities in Strasbourg
that year. This led to battles between Anabaptists and the Holy
Roman Empire in Amsterdam and other Dutch cities.

The second episode of Anabaptist madness broke out
in Münster, where a preacher named Bernard Rothmann
became a secret Anabaptist in 1530. He incited mobs to attack
churches, and began to preach openly Anabaptist views. In
1534 the conflict between the Anabaptists and the Catholic
authorities devolved into violent warfare. This was finally
suppressed by the landsknechts in 1536.

The third episode began in England after the English Civil
War in the 1600s. A novel religious movement known as the

Fifth Monarchists, a millennialist group, became powerful in 1653. It was closely aligned with the Puritans, the first colonists in Massachusetts in 1620.

The Fifth Monarchists predicted an apocalypse in 1667. Charles II destroyed the movement in 1660.

Ch. 5. Miller's Run
(Apocalypse Madness, 1843-1844)

America was destabilised by the economic panic of 1837, following which several schisms opened.

> The early eighteenth and nineteenth centuries saw, respectively, the First and Second "Great Awakenings," religious revivals that swept the United States and England; both spawned a wide variety of unorthodox theologies that, like the Reformation before them, valued individual spiritualism and devalued organized religious hierarchies.
>
> The Second Great Awakening, which was by then already underway, accelerated among the wreckage strewn in the wake of the 1837 panic. Along the way the Awakening midwifed schisms that ranged from Mormonism to blatantly fraudulent spiritual movements like those of the Fox Sisters, whose supposed ability to communicate with the deceased hoodwinked no less than the great author and politician Horace Greeley.
>
> Most spectacularly, as many as a hundred thousand Americans came to believe that the world would end on October 22, 1844, a mass delusion spawned by the most unlikely of millennialist leaders: a modest, unassuming, and thoughtful man

named William Miller.[3]

Miller was active in Vermont, near where I grew up. He was a captain in the Vermont militia at the time of the 1812 war with Britain, and participated in the decisive defeat of the vastly larger British forces on the shores of Lake Champlain. He then became one of Joachim's children. Using number mysticism, he calculated the date of the apocalypse.

> Miller arrived at the startling conclusion of an 1843 Apocalypse. Christ would appear in the clouds and fire would consume the Earth. The righteous — those who believed — would ascend to heaven and immortality, while the wicked would be destroyed by God, who for good measure would eternally imprison their souls.[4]

Miller became fabulously successful, attracting thousands to lectures and camp meetings. The Adventist press published his lectures, and the end date was extended to April 29, 1844. After the Spring Disappointment, further postponements until October 22 and 24 were proposed. Following these October disappointments, the madness faded. Some followers survived and formed the Seventh-day Adventists, which exists to this day, believing in the Second Coming, but without a precise date.

Ch. 8. Apocalypse Cow
(Protestant Mass Mania, 1850)

In this chapter, Bernstein brings the evangelical, (millennialist, apocalyptic, Adventist, second coming, end-times, eschatological) narratives of the past two thousand years up to the present day.

> Over the last half century, a new and highly characteristic form of the end-times narrative now espoused by most evangelical Protestants, "dispensationalism," has given rise to a belief that pervades America and cleaves its society into two camps with very different world views.[5]

This new brand of evangelical Protestantism, aka rapture theology, was popularised in the 1830s by John Nelson Darby (1800-1882).

> This apocalytptic vein of Protestantism only increased over the comiing centuries, reaching a crescendo in nineteenth-century British preacher John Nelson Darby's rapture theology — the premillennial, dispensationalist doctrine that the books of Revelation and Daniel are not metaphor but describe fully literal geopolitical evants yet to come, with 144,000 faithful Christians to be "raptured" or teleported into a tangible heaven prior to a world-ending confrontation between those who are "left behind" and the forces of Antichrist and his one-world government.[6]

A *dispensation* is a divinely appointed order or age. *Dispensationalism*, aka dispensational premillennialism, means a specific end-time sequence:[7] *Rapture, Tribulation, Armageddon*, and *Final Judgement*.

Rapture: The transport of the good/believers/chosen people to Heaven.

Tribulation: The awful period between the Rapture and the

the Second Coming of Jesus to introduce the Advent of the millennial age, when the new dispensation will begin.

Armageddon: The horrible end of the world.

Final Judgement. God decides who goes to heaven.

> This end-times sequence does not conform to the accepted Catholic or conventional Protestant doctrine. Over a century ago most mainstream Christian denominations on both sides of the Atlantic discarded the notion of the Bible's literal truth. In the process, they alienated a significant portion of their flocks; even today, Gallup and Pew polls find that about a quarter of Americans still believe that the Bible is the actual word of God. A similar percentage believe that Jesus will return to Earth in their lifetime, and 61 percent of Americans think that Satan exists, percentages that were almost certainly higher in the early twentieth century.[8]

The seven dispensations currently in use by evangelical Protestants are:[9]

1. *Innocence*, from creation to expulsion of Adam and Eve.
2. *Conscience*, from expulsion to Noah.
3. *Government*, from Noah to Abraham.
4. *Promise*, from Abraham to Moses.
5. *Law*, from Moses to Jesus.
6. *Grace*, from Jesus to the Second Coming.
7. *Millennium*, the final reign of Christ.

We are now in Grace, with no date accepted for the Millenium, beginning with the Rapture, etc.

We may keep in mind this meaning of millenarianism,

or dispensational premillennarianism, in reading all of this chapter. We may now summarize the remaining chapters of Bernstein devoted to relgious manias:

Ch. 9. God's Sword. This relates the history of dispensationalist theology among the Jews, Zionism, and the founding of Isreal.

Ch. 10. Entrepreneurs of the Apocalypse. This chapter is devoted to the extraordinary influence of dispensationalism in the United States today.

> Nowhere is the nation's cultural divide more noticeable than that cleaved by dispensationalism ...
>
> The conventional explanation for the unique, widespread influence of dispensationalism in the United States is that it is more religious than other nations. In 2012, when the National Opinion Research Center (NORC) queried citizens around the world about their religious beliefs, fully 81 percent of Americans agreed with the strong and categorical statement "I believe in God now and always have," versus only 37 percent in Great Britain, 25 percent in Japan, and 29 percent in France.
>
> In the past few decades, religiosity does seem to be waning even in the United States, although less dramatically than in the rest of the world; in 1967, for example, 98 percent of Americans answered yes to the simpler and less categorical Gallup survey question "Do you believe in God?"; by 2017 that number had fallen to 87 percent. ... But while their numbers [of self-identified evangelicals] have decreased [between 2004 and 2018] their influence

has actually increased from 23 to 26 percent of voters, the inescapable conclusion being that evangelicals have more than maintained their political power in the face of declining numbers with increased electoral participation.[10]

Ch. 11. Dispensationalist Catastrophes: Potential and Real.

This chapter explores the relationship between dispensationalism and nuclear catastrophe.

In the early 1980s, novelist Grace Mojtabai travelled to Amarillo, Texas, to investigate the relationship between that deeply religious town and the nearby Pantex plant, which today assembles and maintains the entire American nuclear arsenal. Her magazine piece eventually turned into a full-length book, *Blessed Assurance*. ...

Mojtabai only briefly considered the possibility that religiously crazed Pantex workers might help the millennium along by getting their hands on a nuclear weapon.[11]

Ch. 12. Rapture Fiction (1905)

This chapter is deoted to the history of end-times fiction from its begining in 1905. For example, *Left Behind: A Novel of the Earth's Last Days*, by Tim LeHaye and Jerry Jenkins, 1995, reached the top of the NY Times bestseller list.[12] And *This Present Darkness*, by Frank Peretti, 2002, sold over two million copies.

B. Theories

Psychological theories are presented by Bernstein in the Prelude, and within several chapters. Here we bring together some of these ideas.

On imitation:

> ... our propensity to imitate also serves to amplify maladaptive behaviors, primary among which are delusional beliefs. ... Thus, in the modern world, the tradeoff between imitating adaptive and maladaptive behaviors has become less favorable than it had been in the past, and we are now stuck with a late-Pleistocene imitative predisposition that has become increasingly costly in the modern age, one of the most expensive and dangerous being the spread of the belief that the world will soon end.[13]

On wise crowds:

> Our modern understanding of how crowds can at times behave wisely began in the Fall of 1906, when the pioneering polymath (and cousin of Charles Darwin) Francis Galton attended the annual West of England Fat Stock and Poultry Exhibition in Plymouth. There he performed an experiment in which a large group of people acted with surprising rationality. Approximately eight hundred participants purchased tickets for an ox-weighing contest at sixpence each, with prizes for the most accurate guesses of the weight of the dressed animal, ... Amazingly, the median guess, 1,207 pounds, was less than one percent off the actual weight, 1,198

pounds. The average estimate was 1,197 pounds; …

What separates delusional crowds from wise ones is the extent of their members' interactions with each other.[14]

On the jelly bean experiment:

A few years ago finance professional Joel Greenblatt performed a clever variation on the Galton experiment with a class of Harlem schoolchildren., to whom he showed a jar that contained 1,776 jelly beans. Once again, the average of their guesses, when submitted in silence on index cards, was remarkably accurate: 1,771 jelly beans. Greenblatt then had each student verbalize their guesses, which destroyed the accuracy of their aggregate judgement — the new, "open" estimates averaged out to just 850 jelly beans.

Thus, the more the group interacts, the more it behaves like a real crowd, and the less accurate its assessments become. Occasionally, crowd interaction becomes so intense that madness results.[15]

On confirmation bias (while discussing number mysticism used to predict the end-time):

Number mysticism is inevitably amplified by another well-known psychological phenomenon, "confirmation bias," in which human beings, once they have settled on a hypothesis or belief system, pay attention only to data that support their beliefs and avoid data that contradict it.

The term is associated with a psychologist named

Peter Wason. In a classic late-1950s experiment, he presented subjects with a sequence of three numbers ... and asked them to derive the rule that produced the sequence, and then test it with another sequence.[16]

Conclusions

Part A

The development of the evangelical narrrative experienced a catastrophic bifurcation with the arrival of dispensationalism in the past half century, the time frame of Bernstein's Chapter 8. Its enormous influence upon the political divides of American politics is set out in Chapter B2.

Part B

Evolutionary features such as imitation, confirmation bias, and the jelly bean effect are psychological mechanisms contributing to the madness of crowds. These ideas will be useful in our efforts to use catastrophe theory to model polarization and the onset of civil wars.

Notes

1   Canetti; p. 12.
2   Bernstein; pp. 40-41.
3   Bernstein; pp. 125-126.
4   Bernstein; pp. 132-133.
5   Bernsein; p. 196.
6   Louv, 2018; pp. 21-22.
7   Bernstein; p. 197.
8   Bernstein; p. 197.
9   Bernstein; p. 198.
10   Bernstein, pp. 238, 258-259.
11   Bernstein; pp. 273-274.
12   Bernstein; p. 296.
13   Bernstein; p. 8.
14   Bernstein; p. 11.
15   Bernstein; p. 12.
16   Benstein; p. 131.

Chapter B4
Civil War

Abstract

The culmination of social polarization is the onset of a civil war, a catastrophic bifurcation. For our model of civil war based on catastrophe theory we need to identify two significant control parameters and one measure of the state of polarization. The recent literature of social science provides the crucial ideas. Here we extract them from Barbara Walter's book of 2022, *How Civil Wars Start*.

Contents

Walter's Introduction.
Walter's Chapter 1: The Danger of Anocracy.
Walter's Chapter 2: The Rise of Factions.
Walter's Chapter 4: When Hope Dies.
Walter's Chapter 5: The Accelerant.
The January 6 Committee Report
Conclusion
Notes

Barbara F. Walter, Professor of International Relations at the University of California, San Diego, has written three books on civil war. The most recent, *How Civil Wars Start: And How to Stop Them* (2022), will be our guide to the social sciences of political violence. Here are some selected excerpts from her book.

Walter's Introduction

Here she sets out the frame of the book foregrounding current events in the USA:

> There have been hundreds of civil wars over the past seventy-five years, and many of them started in an eerily similar way.[1]
>
> .....
>
> America is a special country, but when you study the hundreds of civil wars that have broken out since the end of World War 2, as I have, you come to understand that we are not immune to conflict.[2]

Walter's Chapter 1: The Danger of Anocracy.

Here she presents the first of the essential control parameters wew are seekiing.

> Over the past one hundred years, the world has experienced the greatest expansion of freedom and political rights in the history of mankind. In 1900, democracies barely existed. But by 1948, world leaders had embraced the Universal Declaration of Human Rights, which was signed by almost all of the UN member states. It asserted that every person

had the right to participate in his or her government, the right to freedom of speech, religion, and
peaceful assembly, and that they had these rights no
matter their sex, language, race, color, religion, birth
status, or political views. Today, almost 60 percent
of the world's countries are democratic.[3]

The emergence of democracy is a subtle bifurcation. But the
process may lead to a civil war, a catastrophic bifurcation.

It's no coincidence that the biggest civil wars
raging today — in Iraq, Libya, Syria, and Yemen —
were born from attempts to democratize.[4]

Political science has recently compiled extensive data.

There are several large datasets, each measuring
different variables, but most conflict researches tend
to rely on the one that has been compiled by the
Polity Project at the Center for Systemic Peace — a
nonprofit that supports research and quantitative
analysis on democracy and political violence.[5]

And it has developed our first parameter.

One of the most influential measures in the data-
set is called the Polity Score, which captures just
how democratic or autocratic a country is in any
given year. It is a 21-point scale that ranges from -10
(most autocratic) to +10 (most democratic). Countries are considered to be full democracies if they
receive a score of between +6 and +10. ... Norway,
Denmark, Canada — and until recently the United

States — all have a +10 rating. ...

Anocracies are in the middle, receiving a score of between -5 and +5. In anocracies, citizens get some elements of democratic rule — perhaps elections — but they also get presidents with a lot of authoritarian powers.[6]

And the connection between this parameter and civil war.

The CIA first discovered the relationship between anocracy and violence in 1994. ...

The Political Instability Task Force [PITF] ... came up with dozens of ... variables ... and put them into a predictive model. To everyone's surprise, they found that the best predictor of instability was ... a nation's polity index score, with the anocracy zone being the place of greatest danger.[7]

And the implications for the USA.

... according to the V-Dem Institute, another research institute dedicated to tracking global democracy, twenty-five countries are now severely affected by a wave of international autocratization, including Brazil, India, and the United States.[8]

Walter's Chapter 2: The Rise of Factions.

And here we find a related factor, important for the polity index. First, some definitions.

A *faction* is small dissenting group. *Factionalism* is an acute form of political polarization. A *superfaction* is a faction sharing ethnic or racial identity, religion, class, and geographical location.[9] Superfactions are especially dangerous, they can even threaten stable democracies.[10] The Catholics and Protestants in northern Ireland are exemplary superfactions.[11]

In the context of recent civil wars, ethnic and religious factions are the most important.

> In the early twentieth century, when civil wars first emerged as an increasingly persistent problem, most were provoked by ideology or class.[12]
>
> ...
>
> But starting in the mid-twentieth century, more and more civil wars were fought by ethnic and religious groups, rather than political groups.[13]

The PITF found factionalism to be strongly related to political instability and violence.

> Countries that fractionalize have political parties based on ethnic, religious, or racial identity rather than ideology, and these parties seek to rule at the exclusion and expense of others.[14]

So fractionalization is another important parameter related to political violence, and there is a scale for this also.

> Experts assess the level of factionalism in a country based on a five-point scale that goes from a fully competitive political system (5) to a fully repressed system (1). Factional systems receive a rating of 3. (A country's factionalism tracks with its polity index score; as a country becomes less politically competitive, it also becomes less democratic.)[15]

But as the factionalism scale tracks with the polity index, we will use only the polity index as a control parameter in our model.

Walter's Chapter 4: When Hope Dies.

This chapter introduces the role of protests and violent extremism in the onramp to civil wars.

> Violent extremists can also take advantage of peaceful protest movements to sow chaos. Erica Chenoweth calls these people violent conflict entrepreneurs. They try to hijack a social movement by nudging it toward violence.[16]

At this point, Preffesor Walter introduces our second control parameter in the transition to her Chapter 5.

> And in the early decades of the twenty-first century, these extremists who hope to provoke war have an extraordinarily powerful new weopen at their disposal. It's cheap, it's fast, it's remarkably good at generating anger and resentment, and most people are not yet fully aware of its peril: social media.[17]

Walter's Chapter 5: The Accelerant.

This is about the pernicious role of social media.

> Every year since 2010, the world has seen more countries move down the democratic ladder than up it.[18]

...

V-Dem, the Swedish research institute, collects detailed data on the different types of democracies around the world and then rates them on a 100-point scale with 100 being the most democratic and 0 being the least. ... The swift rate of democratic decay around the world has been so rapid that the V-Dem issued its first "Autocratization Alert" in 2020.[19]

It's not likely to be a coincidence that the global shift away from democracy has tracked so closely with the advent of the internet, the introduction of smart phones, and the widespread use of social media.[20]

But social media platforms have proven to be a Pandora's box. The age of information sharing has opened up unmitigated, unregulated pathways to the spread of misinformation (which is erroneous) or disinformation (which is intentionally misleading). ...

As social media penetrated countries and gained a larger share of people's attention, a clear pattern emerged: ethnic factions grew, social divisions widened, resentment at immigrants increased, bullying populists got elected, and violence began to increase. Open, unregulated social media platforms turned out to be the perfect accelerant for the conditions that lead to civil war.[21]

Social media doesn't just drive countries down the democratic ladder. It also heightens the ethnic, social, religious, and geographic divisions that can be the first step in the creation of factions.[22]

Ultimately, it's the algorithms of social media that

serve as accelerants for violence.[23]

The January 6 Committee Report

In January 2023, The Select Committee of the US House of Representatives concluded two years of investigation of the events leading up to the insurrection of January 6, 2021, and issued a report of 845 pages. Then the Washington Post discovered that a draft report on the role of social media in the insurrection, by the Select Committee, existed but had not been released. The Post released it with a comment piece on January 17, 2023.

The comment piece begins,

> The Jan. 6 committee spent months gathering stunning new details on how social media companies failed to address the online extremism and calls for violence that preceded the Capitol riot.
>
> The evidence they collected was written up in a 122-page memo that was circulated among the committee, according to a draft viewed by The Washington Post. But in the end, committee leaders declined to delve into those topics in detail in their final report, reluctant to dig into the roots of domestic extremism taking hold in the Republican Party beyond former president Donald Trump and concerned about the risks of a public battle with powerful tech companies, according to three people familiar with the matter who spoke on the condition of anonymity to discuss the panel's sensitive deliberations.[24]

It seems that the US government was afraid of the social

media giants. The lengthy report by the Select Committee begins,

> Social Media & the January 6th Attack on the
> U.S. Capitol, Summary of Investigative Findings
>
> I. Overview
>
> In the months before the election, President Trump, his allies, other Republican officials, and media personalities across the political right relentlessly attacked the integrity of the electoral process. Large numbers of voters were primed to question the result despite a total lack of evidence of fraud. Years of declining trust in institutions — including the media, government officials, and political leaders — meant no refutation of the "big lie" could loosen its grip on their imaginations.
>
> This is part of a larger trend. For years, observers have warned about the increasing intensity and frequency of Republican politicians' dangerous and incendiary rhetoric. Calls to "take our country back" and warnings of "second amendment remedies" are indicative of a Republican Party that is increasingly willing to use violence to pursue its political ends and increasingly tolerant of extremism within its ranks. Far too often and for far too long, political leaders have capitalized on this escalation instead of confronting it. President Trump's behavior was the culmination of this trend, not its origin.
>
> In recent years, this dynamic has played out on the Internet and especially over social media — though its roots are older than that industry. As

an increasing number of Americans receive news and information online, observers have questioned whether social media platforms have independently contributed to the inflammation of political discourse. Whether or not that is true, social media companies own and profit from the services they provide to users. Regardless of their legal liability, they have an ethical obligation to prevent those services from being used to commit crimes, orchestrate violence, or otherwise contribute to offline harm.

This is true whether or not the attention-seeking, algorithmically-driven business model at the core of the social media industry is driving polarization and radicalization. In fact, the Select Committee's investigation, supplemented by written expert testimony, suggests that shoddy content moderation and opaque, inconsistent policies were a larger contributor to January 6th than the — admittedly not insignificant — challenges posed by recommendation algorithms. As one scholar told the Committee, these algorithms are "just one factor in a broader set of social, economic, and technical issues and incentives baked into the platform[s]."[25]

The 122-page draft report includes extensive evidence in support of these charges. Note that social media not only accelerate the growth of political violence, but also contribute to political factionalization. Deeper analysis of the mechanisms of social media, especially the use of Artificial Intelligence or AI, is presented in the recent book, *The Chaos Machine*, by Max Fisher of the NY Times.

Conclusion

Our first control parameter for our proposed catastrophe theory model for the outbreak of civil war in a nation is the polity index for that nation.

The second control parameter must be some data from social network theory, an index that quantifies the volatility of social media, that is, its effect as an accelerant for factionalization.

And the state of peace or violence in the nation should be an index derived from national statistics.

Now we may go on to these metrics for social media and violence.

Notes

1   Walter; p. xiv.
2   Walter; p. xx.
3   Walter; p. 9.
4   Walter; p. 12.
5   Walter; p. 12
6   Walter; pp. 12-13.
7   Walter; p. 14.
8   Walter; p. 20.
9   Walter; p. 39.
10   Walter; p. 52.
11   Walter; p. 80.
12   Walter; p. 33.
13   Walter; p. 34.
14   Walter; p. 35.
15   Walter; p. 36.
16   Walter; p. 98.
17   Walter; p. 101.
18   Walter; p. 106.
19   Walter; p. 107.
20   Walter; sp. 108.
21   Walter; p. 109.
22   Walter; p. 119.
23   Walter; p. 127.
24   https://www.washingtonpost.com/technolo-gy/2023/01/17/jan6-committee-report-social-media/
25   https://www.washingtonpost.com/documents/5b-fed332-d350-47c0-8562-0137a4435c68.pdf?itid=lk_inline_manual_3, accessed Jan. 18, 2023.

CHAPTER B5
METRICS OF SOCIAL MEDIA

Abstract

Here we turn to the social sciences to search for suitable metrics of social media.

Contents

Introduction

Following our thread seeking control parameters for our cusp model, we arrived at the leading role of social media as an accelerant of polarization. To complete the preparation for our model we need a metric for social media, with data from social science readily available on the internet. Browsing online we find some options.

Adoption rate

From the perspective of network theory, the posting of an innovation by a node precipitates a plume or cascade along edges of the net. Depending on the configuration of the net, the cascade may proceed slowly, then faster, and finally subside as an equilibium is obtained and recipient interest dies. One measure of duffusion over the net is the average rate of growth of this cascade process.

> Adoption rate is a metric used to measure the speed of the diffusion process at a particular time. This metric measures the number of new people who adopt the innovation at a particular time.[1]

We were unable to locate data online of the adoption rate for the major social media platforms, so we may better proceed by first looking for metrics with internet availability.

Data available online

Searching the World Wide Web for social media metrics turns up two good sources: www.datareporter.com and www. statista.com.

Datareporter is an Austrian firm providing data analytics for business. It provides data on the population size of the major social media platforms. For example, as of October 1, 2022, for all platforms:

All users, 7.99B (B for billions),

Mobile phone users, 5.48B

Internet users, 5.07B (63.5% of global population),

All social media users, 4.74B (59.3%),

Facebook users, 2.94B (69% of adult population).

Statista is a German company specializing in market and consumer data. It keeps track of 170 industries in 150 countries. In the social media category, it reports:

Global active users, all social media platforms, 4.7B

Global active users, Facebook, almost 3B,

It collects and makes available a number of metrics, so we may select one of these metrics for purposes of modeling. We choose *global network penetration worldwide* as it shows the size of the maximum recipient base for ultimate diffusion of novel information into the network.

By *penetration* henceforward we will mean this global metric, for all social media.

Penetration

Penetration data is available from www.statista.com for several platforms. We will use the metric for all social media. The annual penetration metric shown today (October 25, 2022) is:

Global, 58.4% (compare Datareporter, 59.3%)

North America, 82%

Statista also provides annual data for preceding years, showing an approximately linear increase from 2018 to the present, increasing from 42% to 60%.

It is this data which we choose for a control parameter of our cusp catastrophe model for polarization. Of course, we cannot control it, it is controlled by another complex system.

Social Bots

Being aware that not all users in the penetration data provided by Datareporter or Statista are humans,we must consider the portion that are not human, the social bot population. This is variously reported as somewhere between 5% and 20% of the total population, depending on the platform. For example, on Twitter it has been estimated between 9% and 15%.[2] We may adopt 10% as an estimate for the present, for all social media.

Conclusion

We are adopting, for purposes of defining our cusp model for social and political polarization and the onramp to civil war, the penetration of human social media use into the global human population, all ages. That is, we propose to ignore the penetration of social bots into the global human population.

This assumes that diffusion over the network is mainly due to human activity, posting and reposting news items. As social bots become more sophisticated, this metric may need to be refined.

To obtain the human penetration data, we must reduce the penetration data provided by Statista by a factor, presently about 10%, to discount the penetration by social bots.

We have not taken disinformation into account, as it does not seem to influence the speed of diffusion of social networks.

In addition to being the control parameter of greatest

importance, it is also a contributing factor to the second control parameter, factionalization.

Notes

1   Information Diffusion in Social Networks, Al-Taie and Kadry, PMC7123536
2   See Wikipedia for social bot.

CHAPTER B6
BEHAVIOR

Abstract

In this chapter we determine the third variable needed for our model of political violence.

Contents

Introduction

We now seek to complete the setup for our catastrophe theory model for the political and social polarization of America, and the onramp to civil war. We need three parameters. These are the two dimensions of the control space, imagined as a horizontal plane, and a mearure of the behaviorf of the system being modeled.

We now have candidates for the two control parameters: political factionalization and social media penetration. There are many other choices, but the utility of our model will not be greatly affected by changing these.

Behavior variables

Finally, we need to settle on a candidate for the third variable required by the cusp catastrophe model. This is the behavior variable, which is to be a proxy for the peacefulness or violence of the country, with data available online.

One possibility is the state of democracy versus autocracy of the government. This might be measured by voting results in periodic elections, considering the platforms running in the election.

An alternative has been presented very recently by the press, in reporting on the attack on Paul Pelosi on October 28, 2022. This is the number of threats reported by members of the US Congress to the US Capitol Police. The data for 2016 to 2021 is shown in Figure B6-1.[1]

What about white power ?

White power, white supremacy, white Christian Nationalism, militias — these movements were fundamental

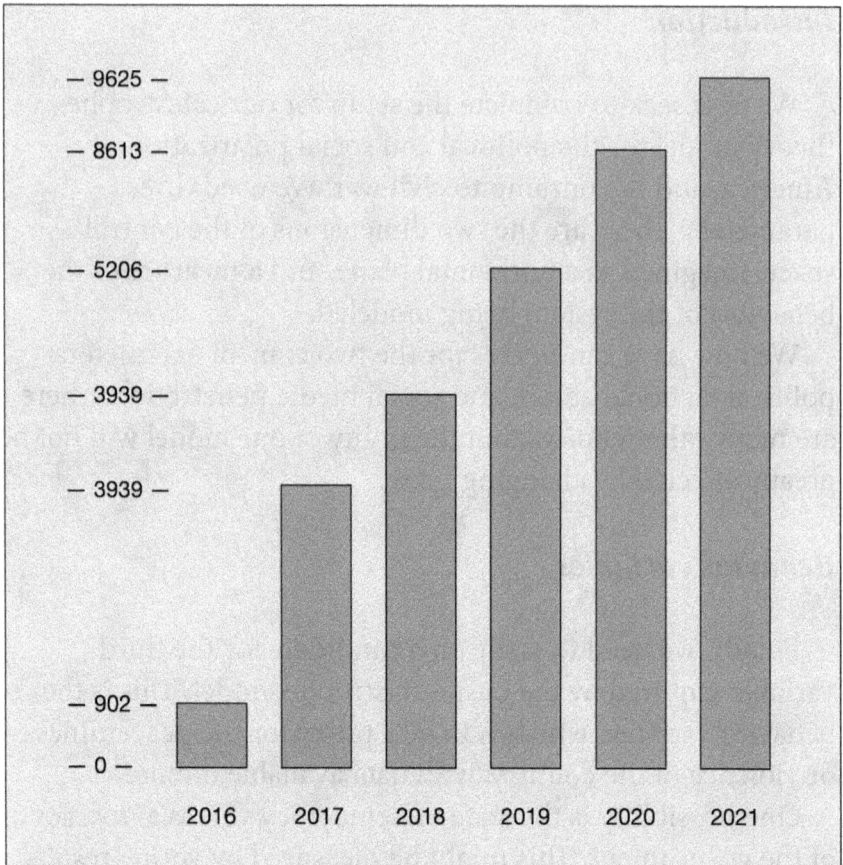

Figure B6-1. Number of threats against members of Congress received by US Capitol Police by year, from 2016.

to the January 6 insurrection. Surely we should consider their strength, or number of members, as a control parameter of our cusp catastrophe model. But we have not found reliable data, updated annually, online.

Understanding white power as a social movement is a project both of historical relevance and of vital public importance. Knowledge of the history of white power activism is integral to preventing future acts of violence and to providing vital context to current political developments.[2]

Conclusion

We now have all three variables identified for our cusp model for political violence.

Notes

1   From the chart by Sarah D Wire, US Capitol Police, House Sergeant at Arms. See abcnews.go.com/ threats-pelo-si-lawmakers-surge

2   (Belew, p. 239)

PART C
CATASTROPHE THEORY

Chapter C1
The Canonical Cusp Catastrophe

Abstract

We are going to create a model based on the canonical cusp catastrophe of elementary catastrophe theory. In this chapter we approach the basic structures of this canonical model with the minimum of mathematical complication.

Contents

Introduction

This is a simple description of the geometry of the cusp model, omitting the mathematical specifics. The main feature of this model is a folded surface in three-dimensional space.

The three variables include two *control variables, a* and *b,* and one *behavior variable, x.* The two control variables define the *control plane, C.*

The Control Plane

The chief feature in the control plane is a curve with a cusp point, called the *bifurcation set.* A bird's-eye view of the control plane, with the axes of the two control variables and the bifurcation set, is shown in Figure1.

The bifurcation set is defined by the equation $D = 0$, where D is the function of the control variables,

$$D(a, b) = 4a^3 + 27b^2$$

This is the curve with a sharp fold, or cusp, shown in gray in Figure 1.

The vertical control axis through the center of the cusp curve, marked a, is called the *splitting factor.* The other control parameter, marked b, is known as the *normal factor.*

The Behavior Axis

The behavior variable is a one-dimensional measure of the state of the system being modeled. It is represented by a point on the behavior axis, a straight line, also known as the *state space* of the system. .

The Three-dimensional Model

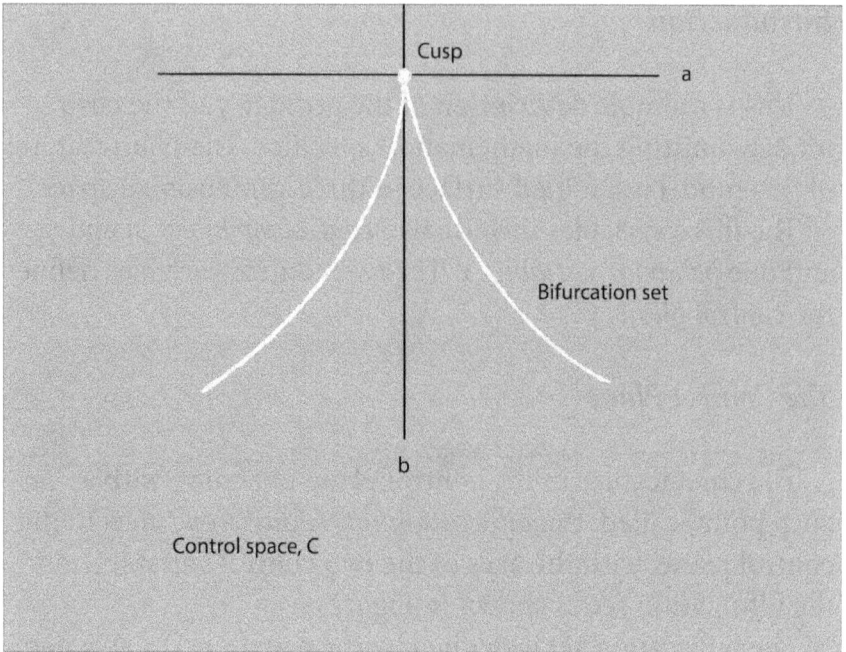

Figure 1. The control plane, C, with white bifurcation set.

We now combine the control plane and the behavior axis into a three-dimensional cube. We orient the control plane horizontally in the center of the cube, and the behavior axis vertically through the origin of the two control axes. The model cube is shown in Figure 2.[1]

For each point in the control plane, C, we imagine a copy of the behavior axis, so a vertical line is attached to each and every point of that plane. The vertical line attached to a point (a, b) of C represents the state space of the system, along with the dynamics of the system with controls set to the values (a, b). Each copy of the state space has its own dynamics, determined by its values of the control parameters a and b.

If the system is started with the initial behavior, x0, then the system will evolve rapidly, with the behavior changing to a point attractor of the dynamic. A *point attractor* behaves as a

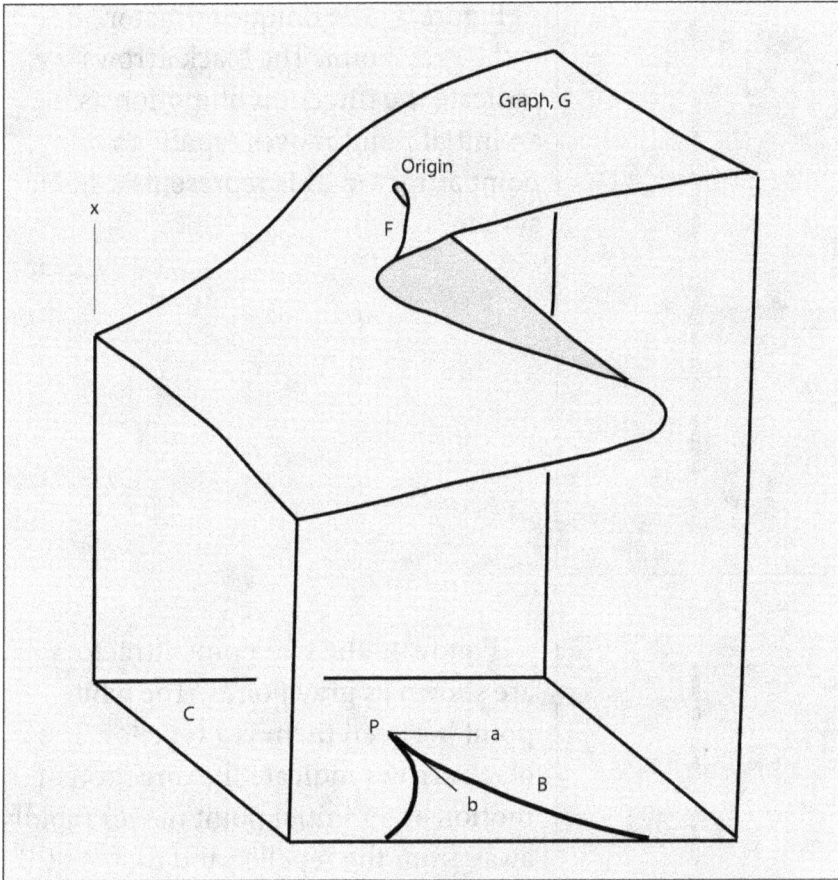

Figure 2. The three dimensional model, with control plane, C, bifurcations set, B, and locus of attraction, Graph, G.

stationary or rest point. The state of the system approaches the point attractor, slows down, and stops to rest there.

All we need to know of the dynamics is the location of the point attractors. There are two cases.

In case the control point (a, b) is outside the cusp curve shown in Figure 1, there is only one attractor, a point. This situation is shown in Figure 3.

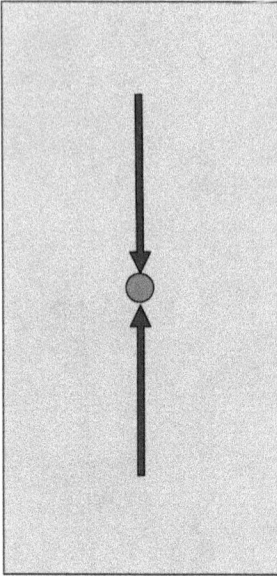

Figure 3. The unique attractor is the gray point. The black arrows indicate the direction of motion as an initial point moves rapidly to the point attractor. This represents a stable system.

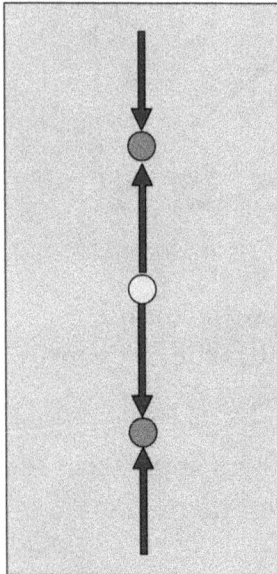

Figure 4. The two point attractors are shown as gray points. The white point between them is a repellor. The black arrows indicate the direction of motion as an initial point moves rapidly away from the repellor and to one of the point attractors. This represents a bistable system, such as a toggle switch.

In case the control point (a, b) is inside the cusp, there are two attractors and one repellor. This is shown in Figure 4.

The Locus of Attraction

We now imagine the behavior spaces, or lines, for *all* control points (a, b), placed within the model cube. We visualize all of the green points, the point attractors, ignoring all other details. The green points sweep out the smooth surface shown in light yellow in Figure 2. Similarly, the repellors, the red points, sweep out the surface shown in darker yellow in Figure 2.

Changing the Normal Factor

The cusp model in catastrophe theory is summarized in the three-dimensional graphic shown in Figure 2. It is especially useful to understand the behavior of the system being modeled when the control parameters are slowly changed. One such scenario is indicated in Figure 5.

Here the control changes from the point labeled A3 in the figure, along the horizontal black straight line in the control plane, to the point labeled A3. Only the normal factor, b, is changed, while the splitting factor, a, remains fixed.

At the start, with control A1, the behavior of the system is on the upper right portion of the locus of attraction, at the point labeled G1. As the normal factor is moved slowly to the left along the black line, moving through the right branch of the bifurcation curve, the attractor slides continuously along the upper sheet of the locus of attraction.

However, upon crossing the left branch of the bifurcation curve at A2, the system finds itself over the edge of the folded upper sheet at G2, far from the only remaining point attractor,

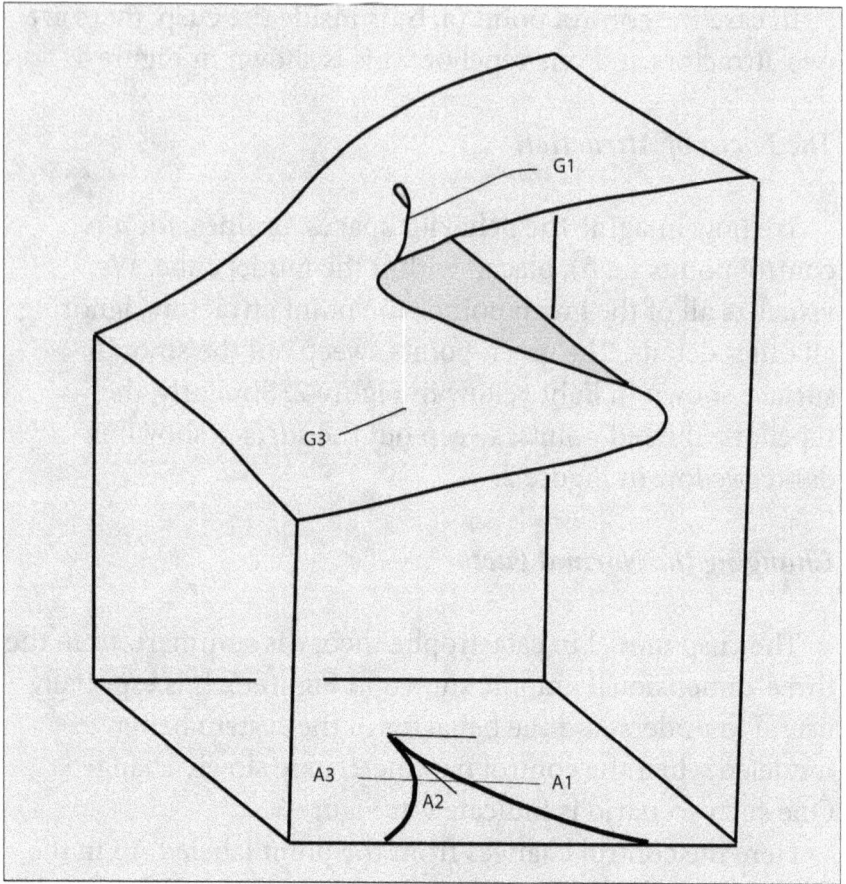

Figure 5. The jump catastrophe as the control point is slowly moved. Here the normal factor, b, is moved from A1 to A3.

which is on the lower sheet of the locus. After a fast jump transition along the vertical white line, the behavior settles down to this attractor. There has been a catastrophic drop in the behavior variable.

As the control continues to the right to the point A3, the attractor slides continuously along the lower sheet of the locus of attraction to the point G3. There are no more catastrophes. This entire scenario is captured in Figure 5.

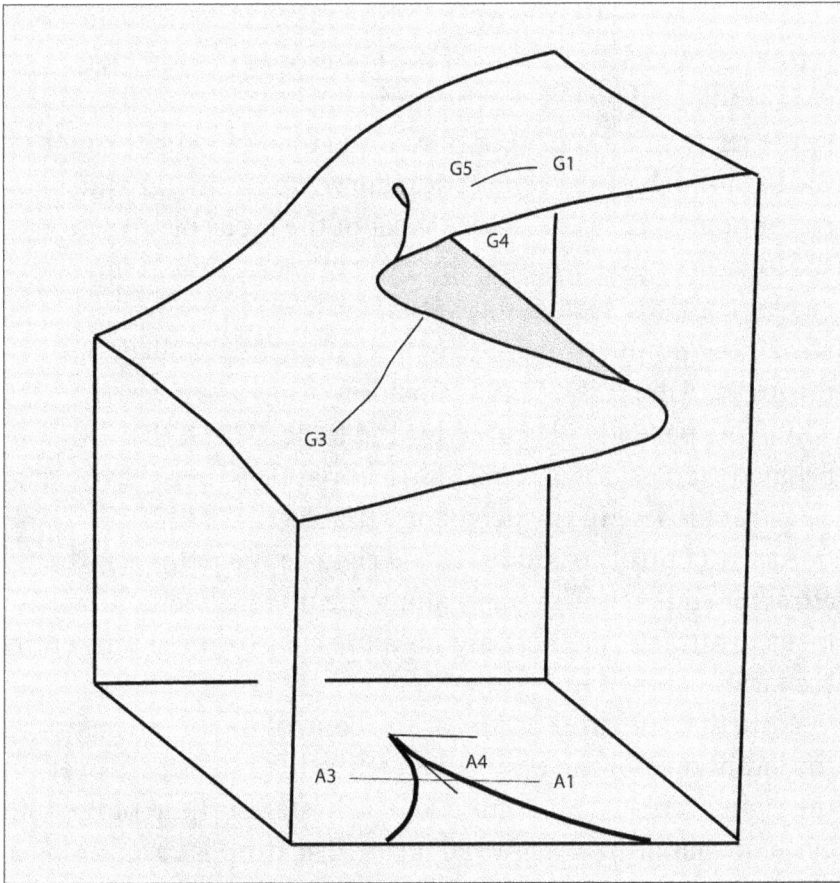

Figure 6. The jump catastrophe as the control point is slowly moved. Here the normal factor, b, is moved back from A3 to A1.

Normal Hysteresis

Now we will reverse this scenario, moving the normal factor of the control point, b, to the right, back along the horizontal straight line, from the point A3 in the control plane to the point A1. Again, the splitting factor, a, remains fixed.

At the start, with control A3, the behavior of the system is on the lower left portion of the locus of attraction, at the point indicated by G3. As the normal factor is moved slowly to the right along the black horizontal line, moving through the left branch of the bifurcation curve, the attractor slides continuously along the lower sheet of the locus of attraction.

However, upon crossing the right branch of the bifurcation curve at A4, the system finds itself far from the only remaining point attractor, which is on the upper sheet of the locus. After a fast jump transition, shown as a vertical white line partially obscured for the folded sheet, the behavior settles down to this attractor at G5. There has been a catastrophic rise in the behavior variable.

As the control continues to the right to the point A1, the attractor slides continuously along the upper sheet of the locus of attraction. There are no more catastrophes. This entire scenario is shown in Figure 6.

Note that the drop occurs as the control moves through the left branch of the cusp curve, while the rise occurs over the right branch. This comprises the hysteresis loop of the full cycle of change in the normal factor. The drop is reversed by a rise, but not at the same value of the control, b.

Changing the Splitting Factor

Visualize a control point inside the bifurcation set, B, near the cusp point, P, in Figure 2. The system has settled down to an attractor, either on the upper sheet or the lower sheet of the locus of attraction. Now increase the splitting factor, a, so the control point moves slowly toward the front of the three-dimensional figure. The system follows the attractor on the locus of attraction, remaining always directly above the control point. In case the attractor is on the upper sheet, the behavior variable, x, increases. On the other hand, if the attractor is on the lower sheet, the behavior variable decreases. The two attractors are split apart increasingly as the splitting factor is increased, hence its name.

Conclusion

The goal of this chapter is to make the primary details of the cusp catastrophe familiar, while holding the math to an absolute minimum. The control plane — with its two coordinates, normal factor, a, and splitting factor, b — appears in Figure 1. The bifurcation set, B, is the cusp curve shown in this figure.

In Figure 2, the control plane appears as a horizontal plane in a three-dimensional space, in which the vertical dimension is the behavior variable, x.

The dynamics in this model are reduced to the assumption that given a point, (a, b), in the horizontal control plane, the behavior variable of the system is at a point in the locus of attraction directly above or below the point (a,b).

The features of this model useful in applications are illustrated in the fast jumps occurring as the control point is slowly moved across the cusp curve, B. These are shown in Figures 5 and 6. These are the catastrophes which give catastrophe theory its name.

Notes

1   Here we follow (Zeeman, 1977; p. 330).

CHAPTER C2
SOCIAL CATASTROPHES

Abstract

Catastrophe theory — originated by René Thom and popularized by E. Christopher Zeeman — provides mathematical models for schismogenesis. Here is a primer on the applications of catastrophe theory to the social sciences by Christopher Zeeman.[1]

Contents

1. Introduction

René Thom (1923-2002) was one of the great mathematicians of the 20th century. He received the Fields Medal of the International Congress of Mathematicians in 1956. Starting around 1966, he developed his interest in algebraic varieties, an important branch of modern mathematics, into a modeling strategy for the sciences he called *catastrophe theory*. The first publication of his theory was a series of papers in the 1960s and early 1970s.

2. Early publications of Thom

The collected works of Thom are being published by the French Mathematical Society in three volumes. The first two appeared in 2017 and 2019. The 2nd volume covers his works from 1962 to1971, and thus includes all his early works on catastrophe theory.

Furthermore, this volume includes a commentary on the genesis of catastrophe theory by Jean Petitot on pages 269-280, entitled, *The first articles by René Thom on morphogenesis and linguistics*. This commentary begins with a list of the five articles discussed, all of which are included in *Volume II* of the collected works. They are:

1. A dynamical theory for morphogenesis, 1967 [47] (English).
2. A dynamical theory for morphogenesis, 1968 [51] (French).
3. Topological models in biology, 1970 [52] (English).
4. A mathematical approach to morphogenesis : archetypal morphological, 1969 [56] (English).
5. Topology and linguistics, 1970 [57] (French).[2]

In addition, the word *catastrophe* appeared for the first time, before his book of 1972, in these four articles:

6. Coupling and catastrophes, 1970 [61] (French),

7. Phase transitions as catastrophes, 1972 [73] (English),

8. Language and catastrophe, 1973 [77] (French), a lecture presented in Brazil in 1971 (I was there), and,

9. A global dynamical scheme for vertebrate embryology, 1973 [81] (English).

In the first of these (pp. 281-296 of *Volume II* of the collected works), we may find formal definitions of *ordinary* and *essential catastrophe points, structural stability, basins,* and *attractors,* as well as the seven elementary catastrophes which formed the basis of the later development of catastrophe theory. The presentation in Volume 2 includes a set of very valuable notes by Petitot.

3. First book of Thom

The theory, along with exemplary applications in various sciences and philosophy, was published in French in 1972 in an important and difficult book. An excellent English translation by David Fowler appeared in 1975.

This book included rather advanced applications of catastrophe theory to diverse areas of physics (breaking waves, phase transitions, diffusion, spiral nebulae), biology (gastrulation, neurolation, memory, mitosis, metazoa), sociology (structure of societies), and linguistics (grammar, language, writing).

4. First book of Zeeman

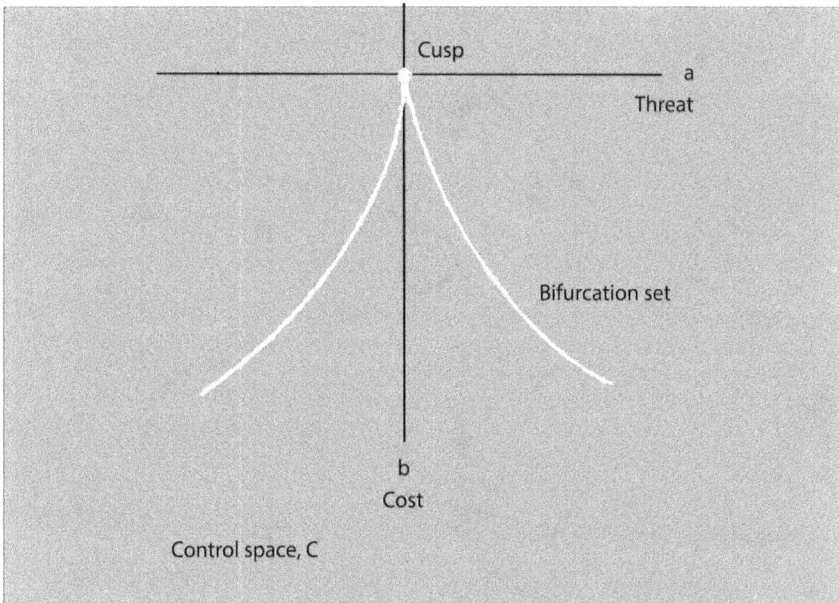

Figure C2-1. The control plane with axes labeled for Zeeman's model for the onset of war. The normal factor, a, measures the perceived threat of war, while the splitting factor, b, represents the assumed cost of war.

Erik Christopher Zeeman, FRS (1925-2016), another great mathematician of the 20th century, excelled in the explanation of difficult mathematics for lay people. He was greatly impressed with the potential of catastrophe theory for new understandings in the sciences, especially the social sciences. In appreciation for this potential, and also noting the difficulty of Thom's presentation of the subject, he undertook a program of popularization of the theory for a scientific audience.

The first publication of Zeeman's program was an article in the *Scientific American* of April 1976. A longer draft appeared as the first chapter of his 1977 book. It included examples presented in clear detail from physics (buckling beam,

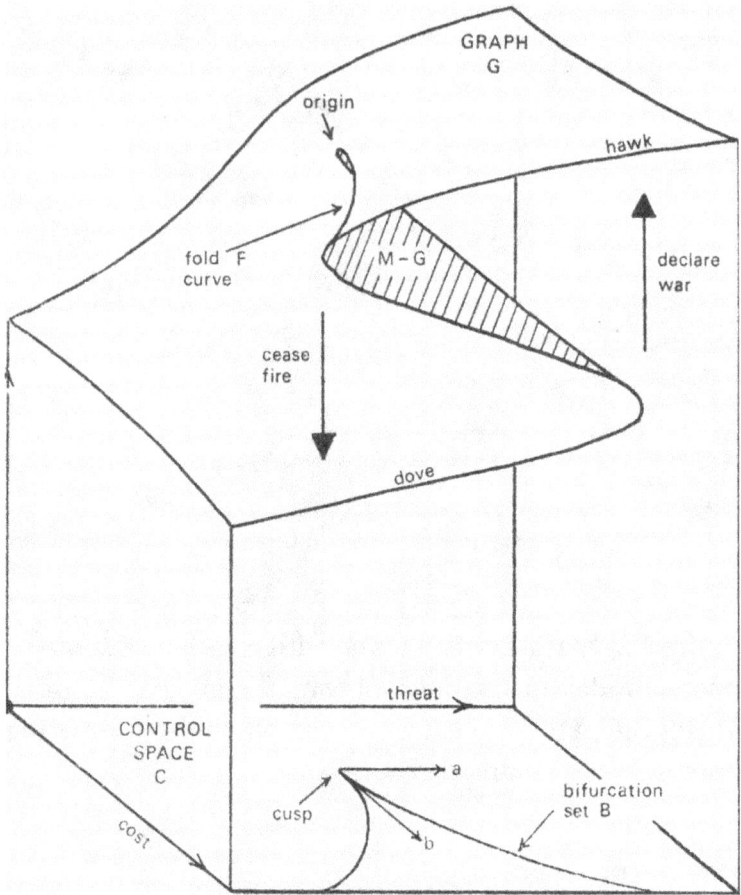

Figure C2-2. Isnard/Zeeman model for the outbreak of war. The control factors are threat and cost. The vertical dimension is the strength of military action.[5]

phase transition), human behavior (self-pity, anorexia), and economics (market crashes).

The book collects his sequel articles from 1972 through 1977. The applications are divided into three sections: Biological Sciences (7 chapters), Social Sciences (5 chapters), and Physical Sciences (3 chapters). In the second of these, Chapter 10, entitled *Some models in the social sciences* (written

with the Brazilian mathematician Carlos A. Isnard), reprints
a long paper (57 pages) originally published as a book chapter
in 1975. This paper had immediate application to arms races,
and sparked a chain of consequent articles.[3]

My plan here is to give a short account of the 1975 paper of
Isnard and Zeeman. In our following chapter, we will discuss
its relevance to the politics of the USA in the years 2016-2022.

5. Public opinion model

The paper of Isnard and Zeeman is divided into 16 sections.
The first section, *The influence of public opinion on policy*,
introduces an exemplary case of the canonical cusp model
described in our preceding chapter. It begins:

> In our first example, we consider the influence
> of public opinion upon an administration, or more
> precisely, the effect that changes in the distribution
> of public opinion have upon the ensuing policy
> adopted by the administration. ...
> The specific example we choose to work with is
> the case of a nation deciding upon its level of action
> in some war, either a hot war or a cold war.[4]

Sections 2-12 explore this model in great detail, using it
as a vehicle to teach the basic ideas of catastrophe theory.
The control factors in this model are shown in Figure C2-1.
The behavior variable is the strength of military action, from
surrender at the bottom of the scale, to strong military action
at the top. The bifurcation set is the cusp curve shown in
white. The three-dimensional representation of this model is
shown in Figure C2-2.

Section 12 considers the changes in military action caused

by different paths of changing control. When a path of control change moves through the bifurcation set, catastrophic changes in military action result, according to the model. We will explain more in the following chapter.

6. Conclusion

Here we have traced the genesis of the cusp model from earliest seed, 1967, up to the war model of Isnard and Zeeman of 1975. In our next chapter, we will edit this model slightly to fit our political situation in the USA in the year 2022.

Notes

1   For the history of the theory, see ch. 1 of this book.
2   Numbers in square brackets are chapter numbers in (Societe Mathematiques de France, 2019).
3   See the bibliography in my MS#54.
4   Zeeman, 1977; pp. 304-305.
5   Zeeman, 1977; p. 330.

Chapter C3
The American Civil War

Abstract

Finally, we adapt the cusp catastrophe model of the preceding chapter to the political turmoil of the United States of America, which appears to be on the on-ramp of civil war in the years 2021-2022.

Contents

Introduction

The cusp model of the preceding Chapter C2 has control factors of Threat and Cost. In Part B we have selected control factors for the American polarization of recent years of Polity Index (proxy for factionalization, from Chapter B4) and Social Media Penetration (proxy for diffusion of information, from Chapter B5).

Likewise, the behavior variable of Chapter C2, Strength of Military Action, is to be replaced by Number of Threats (to members of Congress, as a proxy for level of political violence, from Chapter B6).

Thus our model is obtained directly from that of the preceding chapter by simply changing the labels on the figures.

The adapted cusp model

Changing labels on Figures C2-1 and C2-2, we obtain our adapted model, shown in the two figures here, Figures C3-1 and C3-2. The control factors shown in both figures are Polity Index and Social Media Penetration. The vertical axis in Figure C3-2 represents the Number of Threats to members of the US Congress, as reported by the US Capitol Police.

Changes of control

In our discussion of the canonical cusp catastrophe in Chapter C1, explicit consideration was given to the effects of slow changes in the control factors. For example, suppose the normal factor, b, is set to a position at the extreme right. This means, in our present context (as in Figure C3-1) that the polity index is very high, so also, political factions are

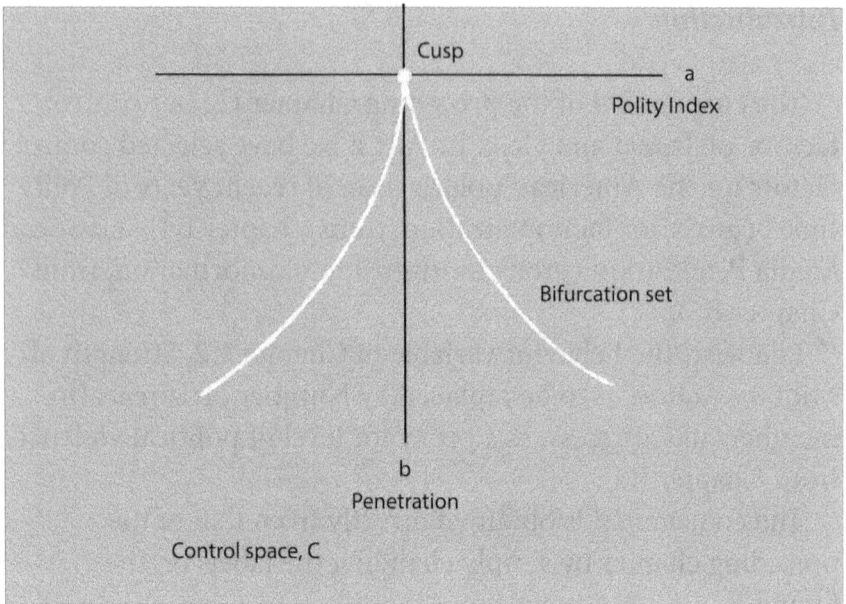

Figure C3-1. The control plane for the adapted model. The control factors are Polity Index as normal factor, and Social Media Penetration as splitting factor.

numerous, concentrated and opposed. Then necessarily, referring to Figure C3-2, that the number of threats to members of congress are high as well, as determined by the hight of the graph, G, in the figure.

Now imagine the polity index being decreased by some news events. As the trajectory of the control point moves to the left and crosses the right arc of the bifurcation set, B, nothing special happens. The behavior variable, Number of Threats, decreases slightly, following a trajectory on the graph, or locus of attraction.

However, as the normal factor continues to the left and passes through the left arc of the bifurcation set, the following trajectory on the graph, G, directly above, reaches the fold curve, F, and drops precipitously to the

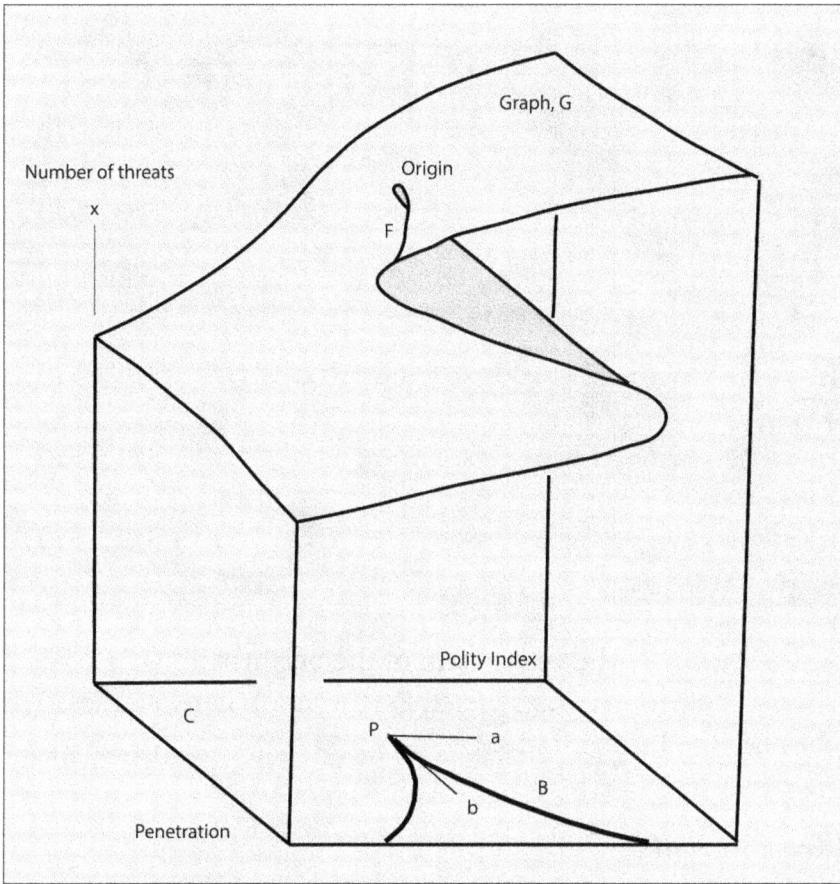

Figure C3-2. The three-dimensional model, adapted to the current context. The three axes have been labeled with control variables: Polity Index (a, normal factor) and Social Media Penetration (b, splitting factor).

lower sheet of the graph, G, as shown in Figure C1-5. This represents a catastrophic drop in political violence. This is a counterintuitive occurrence, suggested by the novelty of the mathematical model.

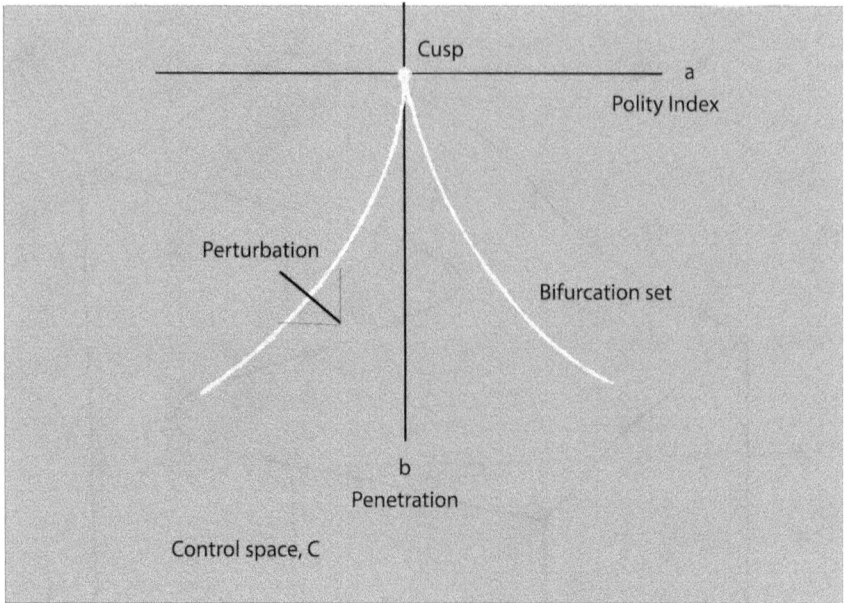

Figure C3-3. The vector sum of the perturbations in the two control factors, labeled Perturbation here, crosses through the Bifurcation set.

Recent events

Consider now the events of November, 2022, in the US. Two special events dominated the news. First, the takeover of Twitter by the industrialist, Elon Musk, on October 27. And second, the midterm elections of November 8.

Interpreting the first as a decline in the splitting factor, Penetration, and the second as a decrease in the normal factor, Polity Index, the combined effect is the vector sum of the two, as shown by the heavy black vector in Figure C3-3. As this control trajectory crosses the bifurcation set, a catastrophic drop in violence is indicated, as in fact occurred following the midterm elections.

Conclusion

This chapter is the culmination of our quest for a catastrophe theory model for politics in the USA. It is also a demonstration of a new way of thinking, using sophisticated mathematics to understand the complex systems in which we live.

Epilogue

In sum, we have delineated the role of AI-algorithmic mechanisms of social media — especially Google/YouTube, Meta/Facebook, and Musk/Twitter — in the rise of political violence. The extensive research of social scientists on this role has been superbly collected and explained by Max Fisher in his book 0f 2022, *The Chaos Machine*.

Selections from Max Fisher

When two scholars analyzed 300 million tweets sent during the 2012 presidential campaign, they found that false tweets had consistently outpaced true ones. The rumors and lies indulged or encouraged anger at the other side, the scholars warned, widening the polarization that was already one of the gravest ailments facing American democracy. [p. 104]

In 2014, ... Facebook's algorithm replaced its preference for Upworthy-style clickbait with something even more magnetic: emotionally engaging interactions. Across the second half of that year ... the platforms in-house researchers tracked 10 million users to understand its effects. They found that the changes artificially inflated the amount of pro-liberal content that liberal users saw and the amount of pro-conservative that conservative users saw. ... . The result ... was algorithmically ingrained hyperpartisanship. [p. 121]

In the coming months [following the 2016 presidential election], digital watchdogs, journalists, congressional committees, and the outgoing president would all accuse. social media platforms of accelerating misinformation and partisan rage that paved the way for Trump's victory. [p. 134]

[Around November 2018] a team of Stanford and New York University economists conducted an experiment that tested, as directly and rigorously as anyone has, how using Facebook changes your politics. They recruited about 1,700 users, then split them into two groups. People in one were required to deactivate their accounts for four weeks. People in the other were not. ... The changes were dramatic. ... overall, the economists wrote, deactivation "significantly reduced polarization of views on policy issues and a measure of exposure to polarizing news." [p. 247]

The day after Biden's inauguration, two Democratic members of Congress [Tom Malinowski and Anna Eshoo] sent letters to the CEO's of Facebook, Google, YouTube, and Twitter. ... "Perhaps no single entity is more responsible for the spread of dangerous conspiracy theories at scale or for inflaming anti-government grievance than the one that you started and that you oversee today."

The letters placed much of the responsibility for the insurrection on the companies. "The fundamental problem," they wrote to the CEO's of Google and YouTube, "is that YouTube, like the other social media platforms, sorts, presents, and recommends information to users by feeding them content most likely to reinforce their existing political biases, especially those rooted in anger, anxiety, and fear." [p. 327

Chaos theory and the Chaos Machine

In this book, *Schism*, we have built a connection between the chaos machine — social media — and chaos theory, an important and little known branch of 20th century math. This connection is a math model for political violence based on catastrophe theory, a branch of chaos theory adapted for applications to the social sciences. Our math model provides a map for strategies to mitigate the epidemic of political violence. The model might be applied to the parallel violent phenomena of racism, gun control, climate change, anti-abortion, covid-pandemic management, police reform, etc.

Our goal, in this lengthy exercise in cybernetic thinking, is to provide clues to a safe and flourishing future for the biosphere and its human population.

After this long wander in three parts through the genesis and development of a new way of thinking based on mathematical modeling and cybernetics, I find myself with this final thought.

The policy-making departments of the US government might make use of this new way of thinking to improve the stability of the United States and thus democracies around the world.

But the chances of this new way of thinking being utilized to make better policies is slim, because the knowledge base required to think effectively this way is too meager. Our educational system has failed us, because the teaching of mathematics is so poor.

REFERENCES

Abraham, F. D. (1990). *A Visual Introduction to Dynamical Systems for Psychology*. Santa Cruz, CA: Aerial Press.

Abraham, Ralph (1967). *Foundations of Mechanics*. New York: Benjamin, 1967.

Abraham, Ralph H. (1981). *Dynamics: The Geometry of Behavior*. Santa Cruz, CA: Aerial Press.

Abraham, Ralph (1994). *Chaos, Gaia, Eros: A Chaos Pioneer Uncovers the Three Great Streams of History*. San Francisco, CA: Harper Collins.

Abraham, Ralph H. ed. (2019). *Hip Santa Cruz 2*, 2nd edn. Rhinebeck NY: Epigraph.

Abraham, F. D., Abraham, R. H., & Shaw, C. D. (1990). *A visual introduction to dynamical systems theory for psychology*. Santa Cruz: Aerial P .

Abraham, R. H., Mayer-Kress, G., Keith, A., & Koebbe, M. (1991). Double·cusp models, public opinion, and international security. *International Journal of Bifurcations and Chaos*, 1, 417-430.

Bateson, Gregory (1936/1958). *Naven: The Culture of the Iatmul People of New Guinea as Revealed through a Study of the "Naven" Ceremonial. Second Edition*. Stanford, CA: Stanford University Press.

Bateson, Gregory (1972). *Steps to an Ecology of Mind: A Revolutionary Approach to Man's Understanding of Himself*. New York, NY: Ballantine Books.

Bateson, Gregory.(1979). *Mind and Nature: A Necessary Unity*. New York, NY: Bantam.

Belew, Kathleen (2018). *Bring the War Home: The White Power Movement and Paramilitary America*. Cambridge MA: Harvard University Press.

Breen, Benjamin, 2019. *The Age of Intoxication: Origins*

of the Global Drug Trade. Philadelphia, PA: University of Pennsylvania Press.

Callahan, J., & Sashin, J. I. (1987). Models of affect-response and anorexia nervosa. In S. H. Koslow, A. J. Mandell, & M. F. Shlesinger (Eds.), *Perspectives in biological dynamics and theoretical medicine, Annals of the New York Academy of Sciences* (Vol. 504, pp. 241-259). New York: New York Academy of Sciences.

Capra, Fritjof (2007). *The Science of Leonardo: Inside the Mind of the Great Genius of the Renaissance*. New York: Doubleday.

Capra, Fritjof, and Pier Luigi Luisi (2014). *The Systems View of Life: A Unifying Vision*. Cambridge, UK: Cambridge University Press.

Carson, Rachel (1962). *Silent Spring. New York: Houghton-Mifflin*.

Eglash, R. B. (1992). *A cybernetics of chaos*. Ph.D. thesis, University of California, Santa Cruz.

Ehrlich, Paul and Anne, 1968. *The Population Bomb*. New York: Ballantine Books.

Eisler, Riane (1987). *The Chalice and the Blade: Our History, Our Future*. New York: Harper & Row.

Fisher, Max (2022). *The Chaos Machine: The Inside Story of How Social Media Rewired our Minds and our World*. New York: Little, Brown.

Fleck, Ludwik (1935/1979). *Genesis and Development of a Scientific Fact*. Chicago, IL: Chicago University Press.

Forrester, Jay W. (1961). *Industrial Dynamics*. Waltham, MA: Pegasus Communications.

Forrester, Jay W. (1961). W*orld Dynamics*. Waltham, MA: Pegasus Communications.

Garfinkel, Alan, Jane Shevtsov, and Yina Guo (2017). *Modeling Life: The Mathematics of Biological Systems*. Cham,

CH: Springer International.

Goodwin, R.(1991). *Chaotic economic dynamic.* Cambridge: Cambridge University Press.

Haraway, D. (1985). Manifesto for cyborgs: Science, technology, and socialist feminism in the 19808. *Socialist Review,* 80, 65-108.

Jung, C. G. (1952/1954/1969). *Antwort auf Hiob/Answer to Job.* English translation by R. F. C. Hull in *Psychology and religion: West and East, Vol. 11. The collected works of C. G. Jung (2nd ed.).* Zurich: Rascher. London: Routledge & Kegan Paul. Princeton: Princeton University Press, Bollingen Series XX.

Karreman, G. (1990). Memories of Rashevsky. *Dynamics Newsletter,* 4, (1), 3-4, (2) 3-4, (3) 3-5.

Kennedy, J., & Yorke, J. A. (1991). Basins of Wada. *Physica D,* 51, 213-225.

Lanchester, F. W. (1914/1956). Mathematics in warfare. Reprinted in J. R. Newman, *The world of mathematics* (pp. 2138-21S7). New York: Simon & Schuster.

Laszlo, Ervin (1987). *Evolution, the Grand Synthesis.* Boston: Shambala.

Lewin, K.(1936). *Principles of topological psychology.* New York: McGraw-Hill.

Lewin, Kurt (1948). *Resolving Social Conflicts.* New York: Harper and Row.

Lewin, K. (19S1/197S). *Field theory in social science: Selected theoretical papers.* West port: Greenwood Press.

Loye, David (1971). *The Healing of a Nation: A psychological and sociological study of racism in the United States, with an original program for political and social reform.* New York: W. W. Norton.

Loye, David, ed. (1998). *The Evolutionary Outrider, The Impact of the Human Agent on Evolution.* Westport, CN:

Praeger.

Loye, David (2007). *Darwin's Lost Theory: Who We Really Are and Where We're Going*. Carmel, CA: Benjamin Franklin Press.

Mar, G., & Grim, P. (1991). Pattern and chaos: New images in the semantics of paradox. *Nous*, 25, 659 693.

Peterson, Erik L. (2016). *The Life Organic: The Theoretical Biology Club and the Roots of Epigenesis*. Pittsburgh, PA: University of Pittsburgh.

Pias, Claus, ed. (2016). *Cybernetics, The Macy Conferences 1946-1953: The Complete Transactions*. Zurich-Berlin: Diaphanes.

Postle, D.(1980). *Catastrophe theory*. London: Fontana.

Rashevsky, N. (1968). *Looking at history through mathematics*. Cambridge: MIT Press.

Saperstein, A. M., & Mayer-Kress, G. (1988). A nonlinear dynamical model of the impact of SDI on the arms race. *Journal of Conflict Resolution*, 32, 636-670.

Societe Mathematiques de France (2019). *Rene Thom: Oevres Mathematiques, Volume II*. Paris.

Strogatz, Stephen (1994). *Nonlinear Dynamics and Chaos: With Applications to Physics, Biology, Chemistry, and Engineering*. Reading, MA: Addison-Wesley.

Thom, Rene (1972). *Stabilite structuelle et morphogenese; Essai d'une theorie generale des models*. New York: W. A. Benjamin.

Thom, Rene (1975). *Structural Stability and Morphogenesis: An Outline of a General Theory of Models*. David Fowler, trans. New York: W. A. Benjamin.

Ueda, Y. (1992). *The road to chaos*. Santa Cruz: Aerial Press.

Waddington, C. H., ed., (1968). Towards a Theoretical Biology. In: *Nature*, v. 218, May 11, 1968; p. 526.

Waddington, C. H., ed., (1972). *Towards a Theoretical*

Biology. Edinburgh: Edinburgh University Press.

Walter, Barbara F. (2022). *How Civil Wars Start: And How to Stop Them*. New York: Crown.w

Wiener, Norbert (1948/1961/2013). *Cybernetics, or, Control and Communication in the Animal and the Machine*. Second edition. Mansfield Centre, CT: Martino. Zeeman, E. C. (1972). Differential equations for the heartbeat and nerve impulse. In: Waddington, 1972; pp.8-67.

Zeeman, E. C. (1976). Catastrophe Theory. *Scientific American*, 234(4), April 1976, pp. 65-83.

Zeeman, E. C. (1977). *Catastrophe Theory: Selected Papers, 1972-1977*. Reading, MA: Addison-Wesley.

INDEX

www.ingramcontent.com/pod-product-compliance
Lightning Source LLC
Chambersburg PA
CBHW072137270326
41931CB00010B/1788